P9-CCX-864

# A Perfect Lawn the Easy Way

# A Perfect Lawn the Easy Way

*by* PAUL N. VOYKIN
*Golf Course Superintendent*
*Briarwood Country Club*
*Deerfield, Illinois*

Rand McNally & Company
Chicago / New York / San Francisco

*To my favorite chess player, Donna*
*and our only treasures,*
*Andrea, Danny, Laura, Linda,* and *Shannon.*


*Library of Congress Catalog Card Number 68-17865*
Printed in the United States of America
by Rand McNally & Company
*First printing, February, 1969*

# Publisher's Foreword

EVERY SO OFTEN a publisher runs into a book that does not classify easily. This is one of them.

At first sight it would seem difficult *not* to be able to classify a book on how to grow a lawn easily and well. But this is *not* the usual book on lawn care. It is different, and it is the difference that makes us want to publish it.

As the author indicates in his Preface, who is better equipped to talk about lawns? It is the man whose job is to satisfy the members of an outstanding golf club that their fairways and greens are perfection itself.

Paul Voykin is an individual. He *likes* to talk about his profession, and he likes to talk about it in his own way. So we have let him do just that, without benefit of ghost or "as told to."

He wants to talk to *you* about *your* lawn. Listen to him—you will profit from it.

*Rand McNally & Company*

# Preface

In *Martin Eden,* Jack London, wrote; "For what reason under the sun do men and women come together, if not for the exchange of the best that is in them. And the best that is in them is what they are interested in, the thing by which they make their living, the thing they have specialized on and sat up days and nights over, and even dreamed about."

Many books and articles have been written on how to grow grass, how to have a better lawn, and the secrets of a good lawn. Although some have been good and some very inaccurate, most have declared it is easy to grow good turf. They have been written by doctors of agronomy and horticulture, who make their living by lecturing and teaching; by landscapers and sod growers; and by fertilizer, chemical, and seed dealers, who derive their incomes from the sale of their products. Of course, gardening editors of newspapers also give advice. However, no book has been written by a golf-course superintendent, a professional who makes his living by growing, maintaining, and supervising the meticulous manicuring of the turf of different heights and varieties that covers the acres of a golf course. He is the man who must keep the golf course in top-notch condition or jeopardize his livelihood. Growing excellent turf is not simple, but it need not be difficult. My profession is grass, and I will try my best to help you grow a perfect lawn in your own yard.

PAUL N. VOYKIN

# Contents

# A Perfect Lawn the Easy Way

# March and April

WHEN SHOULD you start your program of preparing a good lawn? The first day of spring? The first mild day? When you see the first robin? I am convinced that for many homeowners the first urge to start—the first call to action—comes when the beautifully packaged fertilizers and seeds first are displayed by stores, landscapers, and garden centers. But because the successful growing of grass means working with nature and not with the "persuaders," let's keep on the path of common sense. We will start in March, when the signs of spring begin to show and everyone starts thinking about lawns and golf (though not necessarily in that order), but we won't let our enthusiasm carry us too far.

March temperatures fluctuate. Forget them. Do nothing but check the condition of your lawn mower. This step should have been taken in the fall, of course, but invariably the mower is put away dull, dirty, and clogged, and is quickly forgotten—until the last minute in spring. Now, try to start the mower. Most likely it won't work. And if the mower does start, it's probably so dull that it would chew or pull the grass and not cut cleanly. If the mower is completely out of condition, take it to a repair shop. But remember to get the mower overhauled next fall right after the mowing season.

If it doesn't need overhauling then, at least be sure to have it sharpened; this is most important. Lawns cut by dull rotary or reel blades are unsightly because each blade of grass has a ragged, chewed edge—a condition that also makes the grass more susceptible to disease. Everything that you do right can be undone by a dull mower.

Sure, I know the hardware store and the landscaping store, even the drugstores and supermarkets, are displaying all kinds of fertilizers and grass seeds and gardening equipment. Each is in a brightly colored package with alluring, hard-to-resist advertising. Look at them. Price them. But don't be tempted into hauling anything home. So your neighbor is raking and looking very busy. Forget him. He'll catch a cold. Tomorrow it will rain or snow, so let's wait till the ground thaws and the deep frost is really gone. While the cold weather persists, footprints that sink in the muck won't come out with any amount of rolling. Go indoors, look at a seed catalog, watch television, or read Sherlock Holmes. Better yet, learn what you should know about growing a superior lawn. So read on, but forget March.

## Lawn Grasses and Where They Grow

The lawns of today are better kept than ever before. Vast sums are spent on research for better grasses and pesticides to keep them this way. However, the homeowner has to decide what kind of lawn he wants—a hard-wearing, durable lawn suitable for children's romping, wrestling, and playing catch, or a proud showplace for all to admire. Perhaps we can have both. Let's try.

So that you can better understand the turf grasses of Canada and the United States, I am going to divide the area into regions of cool- and warm-region grasses. However, these same regions can be called the great Kentucky bluegrass region (which includes other cool-region grasses) of Canada and the northern United States and the Bermuda-grass (and other warm-region grasses) region of the southern states. The central states comprise a transition zone, too far north for warm-region grasses and too far south for cool-region grasses. In some parts of the area a warm-region grass will do better, in others a cool-region grass; sometimes both will do well. But in this area it is particularly difficult to grow a good turf, because generally grasses are not adaptable throughout the season. (St. Louis, Missouri, is a prime example of a transition zone location.) However, in many local areas one or the other grass will thrive. If you don't have some idea of which grass grows best in your area, talk to the homeowner with the best lawn in your block. I'm sure that he will take great pride in telling you what variety he is growing. Then apply whatever guidelines you need from this book to make your lawn take first prize in your neighborhood.

## Cool-Region Grasses

The major cool-region grass is **common Kentucky bluegrass,** which, incidentally, originated in Europe. There are good reasons for preferring it as the primary turf species in the United States. Its dark-green color, endurance, density of stand, and good texture are only a few of the characteristics that make this *the* grass for the cool, humid regions of North America. Though other excellent varieties are derived from it, the most important being Merion, I call common Kentucky bluegrass the Citation of grasses.

Every variety of Kentucky bluegrass has rhizomes, underground stems thickened by deposits of reserve food material, which help the grass produce a tough sod. Its rate of recovery from adverse conditions is superior to that of many other turf grasses. Kentucky bluegrass is a sun lover and doesn't grow very well in the shade except in the South where, because of the warm climate, it survives *only* in moderate shade. It is susceptible to leaf spot but survives most pests. Its tolerance to drought is also high. It may go dormant in hot, dry weather, but it will start to green up again as soon as weather permits. One year, when it rained off and on all summer, my Kentucky bluegrass rough stayed a beautiful green throughout the season, although it usually goes dormant. The homeowner can keep his bluegrass lawn growing, too, by following proper watering and maintenance practices.

There are many varieties of bluegrass, but in my experience they show little advantage over common Kentucky bluegrass. However, for a new variety to be marketed it should have at least one advantage over other varieties. Here are some of the other bluegrass strains on the market today.

MERION is a widely available variety. As a classic sun grass that will not tolerate shade at all, Merion produces an outstanding lawn with proper care. It is resistant to leaf spot, although it is quite susceptible to rust and powdery mildew. It requires twice as much nitrogen as common Kentucky because of its vigor. Clippings should be removed each time Merion is mowed, and it is important that thatch of plant debris like leaves and stems not be allowed to accumulate on the surface, but be removed by raking. Merion is widely grown in Canada but has lost some favor because of its susceptibility to rust and to winter injury. The desirable qualities of Merion include drought resistance and ability to withstand a short mowing height. In the majority of lawns I've seen I find it is no more drought resistant than other bluegrasses. One of the leading turf nurseries recommends a height of two inches for Merion, and so do I. The care of Merion must not be slackened at any time. It requires regular cutting and maintenance.

The PARK variety represents a mixture of several outstanding selections of Kentucky bluegrass. Park is known for rapid sprouting.

NEWPORT is a selection from the Pacific Northwest. It has a moderately broad, hard, green leaf, and it's also a sturdy fall grass. An outstanding characteristic is strong resistance to rust. However, as years go by, it sometimes thins out and looks ragged.

PRATO forms a dense, fine-textured turf. It will tolerate a rather close mowing height. This new Kentucky bluegrass has some resistance to leaf spot.

Perhaps you are thinking, "Hey, he didn't mention the——— variety! How come?" Well, I didn't forget. There are several varieties of bluegrass I won't comment on because they have little to recommend them. At best they may come close to the ones I have already mentioned. One of the most zealously advertised Kentucky bluegrasses on the market, and extremely overpriced, compares rather poorly with common Kentucky and Merion, both of which are more reasonably priced. However, because of the tremendous sales push on this grass, it is now being widely tested. Until a grass has been widely tested, Mr. Homeowner, watch your pocketbook.

Now, before we get into the cool-region shade grasses, I would like to state that I prefer a pure seed, to give a lawn that classic look.

This elegance never is achieved with a **mixed-seed** lawn. A fancy name on a package of seed may well lead one astray, for frequently the bag contains several kinds of grasses, some of which form a poor-quality turf. However, sometimes there is a reason for mixing species. If, for example, you have trees here and there, casting moderate shade in some places and heavy shade in others, or if your yard is partly dry and shady but wet and shady elsewhere, mix common Kentucky bluegrass with creeping red fescue and *Poa trivialis.* Each grass will dominate where it does best, and you will probably have a good lawn, considering the individual conditions. The other reason for mixing species is to cover a large area, such as an athletic field, a cemetery, or a park, where appearance is not of paramount importance. Here drought-tolerant and shade grasses can be mixed with Kentucky bluegrass. Never use a mixture containing bent seed unless you want a bent lawn. Bent will crowd out all other grasses.

The first of two outstanding shade grasses of the cool humid regions is **creeping red fescue**—tolerant of drought, shade, and poor soil. It doesn't do well when fertilized with too much nitrogen (mixing it with a grass that requires a lot of nitrogen might soon eliminate it), and it is touchy about pest-control chemicals, especially those emulsified in oil. It has fine, dark-green, needlelike leaves, rather stiff and wiry, each rolled tightly together. This compactness conserves moisture and is one reason that fescues are so drought resistant. The leaf when flattened is almost as wide as the leaf of Kentucky bluegrass. I am fond of this grass: it takes such little care and wears so well. It also makes a good sod, and shade doesn't diminish turf quality or density. I'm almost convinced that a 100 percent fescue lawn is as close as we can get to the lazy man's dream of a perfect home lawn, for fescue grows beautifully not only in shade but in full sun.

The other shade grass is **Poa trivialis,** or roughstalk bluegrass, which does well in shady, moist places. The leaves are somewhat like those of Kentucky bluegrass, although they have a shining, glossy, applegreen color. And because the leaves are soft, *Poa-t* doesn't stand up under traffic. Nevertheless, on golf-course fairways that have been mowed at very low heights and watered constantly, this grass has come through some extremely hot periods very well, or, as it's termed in the trade, without going out.

Now, let's look at **bent,** a grass that has had a lot of publicity due to TV and the game of golf. Bent, like a strawberry plant, grows by aboveground runners, or stolons. It is a luxury water grass that does best under ample irrigation. It thrives in places with wet climates, like Great Britain and the Pacific Northwest. Being unexcelled in texture, bent makes a luxurious sward. It can be cut to one-eighth inch, but to look best it requires frequent mowing, top dressing, occasional thinning. It is susceptible to *many* diseases and pests, and unless a homeowner understands its peculiarities and can give it constant attention, he should not monkey around with bent. It is well to remember that luxury grasses requiring a lot of maintenance are likely to look inferior if they're not properly cared for. On a home lawn, bent should be cut at about three-fourths of an inch or lower.

## Warm-Region Grasses

The most important grasses of the southern regions are those of the **Bermuda** family, which do very well in the humid southern states. Their prominence here is similar to that of Kentucky bluegrass in the northern region. Bermuda grass is deep rooted, rather tolerant to drought, and relatively tolerant to saline conditions. It takes lots of nitrogen for optimum growth. As a classic sun grass, Bermuda grows rampant in sunshine, but doesn't withstand shade. Because it spreads by aboveground runners and belowground by rootstocks, or rhizomes, Bermuda is difficult to confine and requires constant edging, frequently becoming a pest in flower gardens, under hedges, and in other cultivated areas. It forms thatch as bent does and shouldn't be cut above three-quarters of an inch; otherwise it will become too stemmy. Like bent, it also needs frequent mowing and removal of clippings for an elegant look. Keep in mind that frequent mowing at proper height is less injurious to the plant than infrequent removal of a large percentage of the leaf area. After a mowing that has been delayed too long, a Bermuda lawn will look brown for several days.

Bermuda was introduced from tropical Africa in the seventeenth century and can be found growing profusely in hot, humid countries, such as India, Uganda, Kenya, Ceylon, and South Africa. Now you know why it won't grow in Walla Walla or Saskatoon—

it needs temperatures of 75° F. and higher to produce the best possible growth.

Several elite, fine-textured hybrid Bermudas are sold. U-3, the oldest variety, has fair tolerance to frost and low temperatures and has been used for northern portions of the Bermuda regions (St. Louis, Missouri). It is coarser than most of the newer varieties. Disease-resistant TIFGREEN is used for the very finest in home lawns and is well adapted for putting greens. However, TIFDWARF, because of its good spring recovery, reduced thatch, and better growth density, is rapidly replacing Tifgreen. Tifdwarf has tiny ground-hugging soft leaves and takes very low cutting. It also produces few seed heads.

In the Deep South and in southern California, ORMOND makes a dark-green lawn that will retain its color late into the fall. Frost-resistant Ormond seldom has seed heads, and under good management it is consistently top quality.

TIFLAWN recovers quickly from traffic damage, which makes it outstanding for athletic fields, campuses, and home lawns. Another fine Bermuda which makes a beautiful lawn is TIFWAY. It is sometimes mixed with Tiflawn to form turf. SUNTURF, an otherwise excellent grass, is rather susceptible to dollar spot.

The homeowner has to realize that the Bermudas must be amply fertilized, cut short and frequently, and their clippings removed. It bears repeating here that thatch, which develops when the clippings are not removed, is closely associated with almost all grass disease.

A favorite grass in the mild coastal areas is **St. Augustine grass.** It is a shade grass of coarse texture with a very attractive dark-green color. It excels in tolerance to salt spray, but must be irrigated. It will also survive cold weather. Brown-patch disease is frequently quite severe on this grass, which may also be hit during the winter. It is susceptible to leaf spot. St. Augustine can't tolerate the arsenates or weed killers of the 2,4-D type. And hold on, the worst is yet to come: the major disadvantage of St. Augustine is a complete inability to withstand chinch-bug invasion.

The chinch bug, a tiny sucking insect, feeds at the base of the grass leaves and attacks the stems. The southern type, Florida's number one pest, has spread wherever St. Augustine grass is grown, causing a great problem for homeowners and ruining thousands of lawns. Since the turf formed by St. Augustine is so dense that chemicals do not readily penetrate its surface, the best treatment is intensive aerifying to let chemicals mixed with wetting agents make contact with the base of the soil and nail the bugs. These chemicals must be switched from time to time so the chinch bug can't develop resistance to them, which is its successful survival tactic. To get down where the bugs live, a sprayer should be powerful enough to penetrate this tough turf. The minimum pressure needed is 200 pounds per square inch. Use of the most potent chemical against chinch bugs, parathion, has a drawback: it is a poison that affects the central nervous system of human beings. Therefore, parathion should be applied only by licensed specialists. Homeowners should use a safer chemical, like Malathion. Chlordane, in contrast to its success against other insects, won't even make the chinch bugs sick.

Nevertheless, St. Augustine is still very popular for its good characteristics, and in Texas and Florida it is used in 50 percent or more of all home lawns.

Two other popular southern grasses are **centipede grass,** introduced from China, which likes to crowd out everything else, especially in a pasture, and **Bahia grass,** which is the only grass centipede can't crowd out. Both are of intermediate quality, require but little fertilizer, and can be cared for easily.

The last elite southern grass, one used especially in the transition zones, is **zoysia,** a native of Asia and formerly known as Korean or Japanese lawn grass. This grass has a tremendous root system and forms a dense sod. It spreads the same way that Bermuda does, by rhizomes and stolons. It is extremely resistant to wear but recovers slowly when excessively damaged. Zoysia is drought resistant and completely crowds out crabgrass and other weeds, especially the broadleaf varieties. It needs less attention than Bermuda once a sod forms. Two disadvantages of zoysia are its very slow start and its even slower spread. Two years or more are usually needed to form a satisfactory sod, depending on soil, climate, and planting practices. Transplanting is a critical time for zoysia, and care during the first week is crucial for its survival. Then it takes at least twenty-one more days to recover and start spreading. During the first year or two weeds present a problem. Zoysia is hard to mow, especially if mowing is delayed, so make sure your mower is always sharp.

Around Kansas City and St. Louis, zoysia has become the favorite grass. Among its varieties are MIDWEST (coarse), MEYER (medium), and EMERALD (fine). If you live in Chicago or other areas of similar climate and hate cutting the grass (who doesn't?) and don't care what your neighbors think, go ahead and try a zoysia. Your grass, when it gets started, will green up in May and turn brown in October. (It can become a fire hazard when very dry.) Therefore, you won't have to cut until the middle of June and you'll be set through September 1. Isn't that wonderful! Of course, much of the time your lawn will be the color of straw. In the North it does not tolerate shade. Zoysia received much publicity and advertising when it was introduced in the early 1950's. The hucksters would like the public to believe it's a miracle grass and a panacea for all lawn problems, but much of the advertising is misleading, particularly when it's directed to the northern homeowner.

Before leaving the discussion of southern grasses, I must give some advice on **overseeding,** which can be done anytime from October to December with cool-region winter grasses. Overseeding means simply the spreading of rye seed on existing grass to make the lawn green. The exact day, week, and month will depend on your location. For best results, prepare to aerify your lawn in two different directions before seeding. The aerifying machine relieves compaction and opens up the thatch. Next, set your mower down to half the normal height, cut the grass in two directions, and pick up the clippings. Then seed the lawn. Finally, hand water to wash the seed into the soil. The lawn can be drag-matted and, if this step isn't too expensive, sometimes topdressed. A homeowner should be cautioned not to burn his lawn with flame before seeding, as some golf-course superintendents do, to get rid of thatch and mat. He might burn more than just his lawn. Excessive thatch can be removed mechanically by two methods: verticutting, in which the thinning is done by a vertical-bladed lawn mower, and aerothatching, which makes slits in the soil and removes matted grass. But this is a job best turned over to a qualified landscaper who has the expensive machinery and experience to do this difficult operation.

The most popular seed for winter overseeding is rye. It is plentiful, cheap, and compatible with St. Augustine and centipede grass, and it germinates in three to seven days. Rye grass is susceptible to diseases like dollar spot, rust, and damping-off, but the University of Florida has developed a rust-resistant strain of rye grass that has many advantages over the old type. Other cool-region grasses have been used with great success to overseed in some areas, although they take longer to germinate. A mixture of *Poa trivialis,* red fescue, and Kentucky bluegrass is often used as an alternate of rye grass.

The most important factor in the success of an overseeded winter lawn is keeping the seedbed moist so the grass will grow rapidly. Because zoysia and Bermuda turfs grow so densely, a satisfactory stand of overseeded grass is especially difficult to get. Therefore, attention to seeding and maintenance is needed to help ensure success in getting a winter lawn.

## Prairie Grasses

The discussion of grasses for home lawns is over, except for those grasses I am most fond of. I speak of the prairie grasses, and as I write this I remember the prairies, with their undulating waves that were like soldiers bending into the rush of an attack, then being subdued for a moment before bending forward again as the great general of the plains, the prairie wind, waved them onward.

As a young boy I lived in Red Pheasant, Saskatchewan, one mile from a Cree Indian reservation. Here was my first experience with turf, for we lived a short time in a house made of prairie sod, jokingly called Saskatchewan brick. The only trouble came when a wagon bumped into it—or even rode close to it—and dirt would spill into the "living room." But boy, was it warm in winter!

My father did business with the Indians and traded everything from freshly baked bread to leather harnesses. Well, almost everything. An Indian named Charley Two Bears became quite fond of me and offered my father ten wagons of hay as fair trade. My father later teased me (I think) by saying that he would have traded me if Charley had offered a little more. Even so, the fragrance of freshly cut prairie hay has special, wonderful memories for me. It's sad to think that other children will rarely see these prairie grasses and that their children will know them only from pictures and stories.

Today these prairie grasses are used primarily for hay, pasture, and erosion control. Among the many varieties of cool-region prairie grasses are the crested wheat grasses, orchard grass, timothy, porcupine, and blue grama grass. The bluestems, buffalo grass, and the gramas are the warm-region prairie grasses.

## Lawn Diseases

At this point I should follow the procedure of other books and articles on lawns by listing all the turf diseases and outlining ways to recognize and cure them. Well, I'm going to describe only the principal lawn diseases because, with the limited information available, the average homeowner wouldn't be able to diagnose with certainty the disease hurting his lawn, no matter how many pictures and descriptions he had in front of him. Unless the disease can be correctly diagnosed, any haphazard attempts at treatment will result in wasted time and money, possibly even further injury to the lawn turf. In my experience as consultant, 99 percent of the lawns described by homeowners as being riddled by disease were not diseased at all. However, the thing to bear in mind is that the natural color of a healthy grass blade during the growing season is green. That's the key. If the blade is any other color, it might be suffering from too much or too little watering, improper fertilizing, chemical burn, mower damage, or even insect damage. If it has purplish-red or brown or black spots or lesions along the sheath, it is diseased.

A golf-course superintendent has learned to identify the different turf diseases only after a very long time, and even then he has difficulty in recognizing some of them and prescribing the proper treatment. You see, turf-grass diseases vary in severity from year to year and from one locality to another, depending on temperature, shade, moisture, humidity, type of grass, and grass nutrition. Over a hundred fungi attack turf grasses and cause a diseased condition, and these are usually more evident on a golf course than on home lawns. However, it's safe to say that one of the turf-grass diseases strikes every lawn in North America at least once during the course of the growing season without the homeowner's even knowing that his grass is in trouble. Fortunately, the grass usually recovers by itself when the weather changes from hot to cool and from wet to dry. It is well to remember that high temperature and humidity bring on the most rapid fungus action; dry air discourages the activity of the parasitic fungi. The golf-course superintendent is most vigilant during the "jungle days" of summer, watching his turf, particularly extremely low-cut turf like the bents and Bermudas. Home lawns, though mowed much higher, are vulnerable to fungi at this time.

Fungus is easily spread by wind, water, and grass clippings. You'll often need to purchase a chemical fungicide to help your grass. Lawn and garden centers can recommend and supply these chemicals. Apply the fungicide twice, allowing a week between applications. Add one tablespoon of household detergent per gallon of water mixture; this will help spread it over the leaf blade. If grass is undernourished, applications of fertilizer, as recommended on the bag, usually will help keep a fungus from becoming epidemic. But before you resort to chemicals, try removing the early-morning dew with swipes of a bamboo fish pole or by dragging a loop of garden hose across the lawn. It helps to dry the grass.

However, before diseases are blamed for the lawn difficulty, be sure the lawn isn't in need of water or fertilizer. Perhaps it's just been injured at the tips by a dull mower. Remember also that certain varieties of bluegrass and some other grasses tend to go dormant in hot, dry weather. It certainly isn't uncommon for a lawn to become brown from lack of water in the summertime. You also can check possible damage from dog urine or from gasoline leaking out of your mower.

## Identifying and Controlling Fungi

Now I'll describe some of the major lawn diseases so you can recognize them easily. A lawn given proper care and maintenance should not have serious disease problems. The diseases that usually attack a home lawn are fairy ring, powdery mildew, leaf spot, rust, and snow mold. Brown patch and dollar spot will attack bent lawns and such southern grasses as Bermuda and St. Augustine. Occasionally in northern regions the bluegrasses will also be struck by brown patch and dollar spot.

**Fairy ring** is usually associated with childhood stories of little people dancing by the light of the moon. Wherever their feet touched, mushrooms were supposed to grow. The story has charm, of course, but fairy ring is a fungus disease. It may have a diameter of a few feet, or, as I saw once in Lethbridge, Alberta, it may have a diameter of almost a mile. Some growths have been found to be hundreds of years old. Fairy rings can be either dark-green circles of stimulated grass or rings containing different species of toadstools or mushrooms, some of them edible. Don't take a chance; pick the mushrooms up whole and throw them away before children get curious and get to them first.

Fairy rings are difficult to get rid of once they get started. Therefore, a good management program is more practicable. Water properly, fertilize adequately, and remove the thatch several times a year. Do this, and the fairy-ring problem will be lessened.

Fairy ring causes soil to be very dry, especially during the summer. Actually it's a localized dry spot caused by fungus mycelium, whose habitual branching of filaments "cements" the soil and excludes all water. Although the disease usually is noticeable only during the summer and fall as a dead ring, in the spring it may occur as a dark-green ring because it's stimulated by the nitrogen from the decayed grass roots.

There's one treatment you can try before others. With a narrow penetrating tool, punch holes one foot deep and one foot apart both inside and outside the circle. Flood them with water every day for a week. If the ring is larger in diameter than your height, use a small posthole digger and dig the holes two feet deep and two feet apart inside and outside the circle. Flood for a week, then fill the holes with fresh dirt and seed them. These methods don't always work, but they do halt the progress of the fungus. I recommend these treatments rather than messing around with fungicides. However, the best method is to attach a tree-root feeder to the end of a hose and insert it into the ground, circling the ring as I've described above. But if you really have a monster of a ring, call a tree-service expert and have him soak it with a powerful root feeder.

**Powdery mildew** is most severe in shady areas. Its primary target is Merion and other varieties of Kentucky bluegrass in dense shade under trees, beside shrubbery, or on the sunless side of your home. The grass will look as though it's been sprinkled with flour or face powder. Once under attack, the grass deteriorates rapidly. You can prevent this disease from becoming a serious problem by growing shade-tolerant grasses or ground covers. If powdery mildew is anticipated, I would advocate mixing Kentucky bluegrass with other grasses because the mixtures seem to survive better. Injury to the bluegrass is masked by the green leaves of the nonsusceptible grasses. Pruning dense trees and shrubs to improve air circulation and reduce shade also helps keep this disease in check. In addition, I strongly recommend that all clippings be picked up when you mow until the grass becomes healthier. In fact, I suggest you do this whenever your lawn has any disease.

**Leaf spot,** melting-out, foot rot, and fading-out are names commonly given to the disease whose technical name is helminthosporium leaf spot, after the fungus. Merion bluegrass is highly resistant to this blight, while common Kentucky bluegrass is sometimes badly injured. Leaf spot usually becomes worse during prolonged periods of wet, humid, cool, sunless days in spring and fall, or when the grass is kept continually wet by frequent light sprinkling, which, for the record, is one of the bad habits of the American homeowner.

While we're on this topic, let's take a closer look at some of the disease problems associated with watering practices. The longer the grass is wet, the greater the chance of disease. Of course, if it rains continually for a long period, we can't help that, but it might be wise to spray with a leaf-spot fungicide right after the rains stop. Be sure to observe label directions when using any fungicide; if they are not followed properly, you might as well not use the fungicide.

The best control for leaf spot is to spray two times with a fungicide in early spring, allowing two weeks between sprayings. Don't cut lower than two inches. Fertilizing also keeps the grass healthy and enables it to recover from leaf spot by itself; if it's undernourished, it may not. Don't worry about leaf spot in the fall because it hardly ever becomes serious then, and chemical control is seldom necessary. Leaf spot is one big reason for not fertilizing too early in a wet spring, as some of the leading fertilizer companies encourage us to do. Fertilizers, particularly if they are heavy in nitrogen, produce luxuriant grass which is especially susceptible to leaf spot.

**Rust** usually doesn't appear as a problem until August or September, after long periods of hot, dry weather when the grass is nearly dormant and growing slowly. This fungus has appeared as early as June in the central and southern states, though. It is more noticeable on Merion bluegrass than on any other variety of Kentucky bluegrass, and, because of this susceptibility, a few areas favor common Kentucky bluegrass. The rust gives grass a reddish-brown, reddish-yellow, or orange-yellow appearance. The spores will even collect on your shoes and turn them the color of the spores.

The best control is fertilizing and watering to cause new leaves to grow. Since Merion thrives on a fertilizer program with higher nitrogen content than do the other Kentucky bluegrass varieties, you're accomplishing two things at once—turf nutrition and disease control. There are chemicals that control rust on Merion, common Kentucky, and other grasses, but these must be applied repeatedly and are quite expensive. Fertilizer is your best bet, but don't burn your grass with it. And after you mow be sure to pick up the clippings. This sanitation practice applies to all turf diseases.

**Brown patch** is a fungus that most readily attacks the bents in the northern regions and such southern grasses of the United States as Bermuda. It is especially tough on shaded St. Augustine grass. Brown patch infests grass that has become thatched and somewhat lush, particularly when the days are warm, wet, and humid and the nights are warm and muggy. This disease wilts leaf blades inside an irregular brown circle, which often has a smoky ring around the edge. The patch or patches develop very rapidly, frequently attaining a diameter of two feet or more overnight. The fungus growth stops and the grass recovers as soon as the weather cools and becomes drier. If your lawn is cut as short as golf-course turf, you'll have to spray regularly to prevent the disease. Several of the newer fungicides are relatively safe to use and yield outstanding control of this disease.

**Dollar spot** looks like—well now, take a guess. I call it the cold sore of the turf diseases. It is most prevalent on bent grasses, rye, and St. Augustine grass, and it first appears during the cool nights and warm days of springtime. The two-inch spots are first a grayish, woolly white, caused by the cobwebby mycelium of the fungus. Then they become bleached or straw-colored. The cobwebby film can be seen in the early-morning dew. Although dollar spot has been considered mainly a problem of spring and fall, it can be serious in summer, too. With bent grass, this disease should be considered a potential problem throughout most of the growing season. The owner of a bent lawn usually will have to spray with the same fungicides used for brown patch, thereby controlling both diseases at once. Dollar spot becomes most severe when there is a deficiency of nitrogen. I usually begin looking for signs of the fungus during the first week in June.

**Snow mold** exists in gray and pink varieties. Both snow molds develop under the winter snow cover. In the spring, as snow melts, the fungus causing snow mold covers the grass with a cobwebby growth that is very noticeable. The spots—white, pink, reddish white, or dirty gray—will appear along fences or in shady areas. They will frequently occur where the snow has been packed, in such areas as paths trampled by foot traffic. Snow mold is the most devastating turf disease on home lawns in Canada, although a few native varieties of bluegrass have some natural resistance.

Apply a snow-mold fungicide in late fall or early winter. Control materials are readily available in lawn-supply stores. In Canada, apply fungicide in early fall, well before the first snow. This is important because, in most of Canada and the extreme northern sections of the United States, snow remains on the ground into late spring. In the Midwest, I would suggest application of the fungicide after the fall season's first snow, which always melts. Do not allow the grass to enter winter in a lush condition, for this may not only cause snow mold to be more of a problem but may also cause increased winterkill, or suffocation of the grass, especially if the winter is a long one. In spring, snow-mold spots that reach a foot in diameter may be raked or poled to remove the cobwebby, crustlike growth. The grass may recover if still alive, as some of it usually is.

Well, that's it for lawn diseases. Those I've described are the most common. However, in recent years a few new ones have cropped up that are considered major headaches. These include spring dead spot, a serious enemy of Bermuda; ophiobolus patch, which invades the bent of the Pacific Northwest; and fusarium blight. There are no proven controls for some of these.

If you want more information, or charts and pictures, write a letter to your county agricultural agent, the farm extension service, or the college of agriculture of your state university. It costs only a little more to phone your municipal or private golf course and talk with the superintendent if you are in real trouble. In some cases, you may want to hire a professional turfman as consultant. And for the price of a short drive in your car, why not take him a sample of the problem grass?

Now we come to April—a restless time—and it's impossible not to do something. The yard bug has really got us.

Let's begin.

## Lawn Cleanup and Small Chores

Now that the lawn is drier, give the grass a good combing. The purpose is to straighten the grass that was matted and half smothered by the heavy snow all winter—mostly because you didn't mow in late fall when the grass was so tall. Another reason for raking is to clean from your yard all debris, from branches to dog dung, that has accumulated since last fall. The third reason is that raking helps collect the dead grass; this not only aids in preventing the grass from forming thatch but stimulates growth. Most important of all, though, your yard will be neat. Check again for litter. It's simpler to pick up a piece of paper on the lawn once rather than twenty times after your mower has gone over it. Go in now and have a beer, or gab with your neighbor about whether Chicago is going to win the Stanley Cup.

## Tools and Birdhouses

If you'd rather be outdoors, go back into the garage and check the tools. If they're broken, repair and paint them. Keep everything hanging on the wall so your car doesn't run over them.

How about your birdhouses? Have you looked at them? Although I'm in favor of birdbaths and feeding stations for birds, especially during hard times, I like to see my cardinals, bluebirds, and chickadees against either a white snowbank or a background of green or gold. But if you have these fancy shelters, this is the time to clean and repair them. They'll probably need a fresh coat of paint, too. Be sure they're completely dry, though, before replacing them.

Early April is a good time to work on your trees. There's some information about them beginning on page 103.

## Mowing

When the grass has really started to grow you begin to think about mowing.

If the mower is ready, tell the mechanic to be sure to set the cutting edge at two inches if you have common Kentucky bluegrass or one of its varieties. Then have the reel and the bed knives set so all of the blades cut newspaper. The rotary mower will do a satisfactory job if the blade is always sharp. This is the secret of a good lawn cut by a rotary. The reel mower is more expensive and naturally is costlier to overhaul, but it cuts more cleanly, like scissors, and the difference is quite noticeable. We'll discuss mowers in greater detail on page 72. For the present, let's get along with the one we have.

Your grass should be cut now that you're ready. Use the catcher only in the spring, when the grass is growing vigorously, and again later on in the fall. However, if your lawn is of bent, Merion, or Bermuda, use the catcher each time you mow, because otherwise the thatch will become a problem; the accumulated cuttings of these grasses cause poor soil drainage and air ventilation and provide perfect conditions for disease to begin. More information on mowing on pages 39, 63, and 78.

## Checking the Rainfall

We are approaching the last of April, and the persuaders are all around you, including some of your neighbors who already have fertilized and seeded the open spots on their lawns. Fertilizing the lawn during the last part of April is permissible, seeding never; so let the persuaders go ahead. Remember, we are after a perfect lawn and nothing less.

The best thing you can do is to go to the store and look at everything again, but buy only what you will need to repair your tools and lawn equipment. Wait a minute. Buy a rain gauge and set it somewhere in your yard, maybe next to your birdbath. Then when you're measuring next night's rainfall, you may notice the birdbath needs cleaning. With a rain gauge, you will know exactly what your area receives in total rainfall. Keep in mind that the official measurement at the recording station is not always what your area receives, and rarely so if you live in the suburbs. You will learn from the different amounts of rainfall how long the ground takes to dry and when you will have to water again, or when you can safely plan for a lawn party. One inch of rain registered on your gauge might last two weeks or only one week, perhaps less, depending on the condition of your soil, the wind, humidity, temperature, the height of cut, the part of the country in which you live, and the general health of your grass. I'm sure you're aware that the lawn's moisture requirement is quite different in the spring than during the stress periods of the hot summer. But one thing you can be sure of—when the grass starts to brown, when the ground becomes hard and a bit of it crumbles in your fingers like sand, that's the final big test; that's when you water again, and water heavily.

## Preparing for Fertilizing

Check your fertilizer spreader. This is very important because most lawn burns result from improper calibrations of the spreader. Usually too much or too little is spread because the setting is way off, and then the fertilizer is blamed.

It's a good time now to measure your lawn properly, once and for all, in square feet. Most people know the capacity of their refrigerators, swimming pools, and water heaters; they know the area of their room rugs, but not of their lawn. Be sure when measuring to subtract the house, garage, and other large areas that aren't grass. By having someone help, you can double-check each other's lawn measurements and know exactly how much fertilizer to order. We don't wish to pinch pennies, as did Henry Thoreau when he was at Walden, but let's be a little frugal. Besides, why clutter your garage with too much?

Most instructions for the use of fertilizer are based on an area of 1,000 square feet. To get an accurate calibration, go out and measure 1,000 square feet, or 500 square feet on the asphalt drive, even the sidewalk. Then work out the proper setting on your spreader for 1,000 square feet. If the recommended rate is 10 pounds per 1,000 square feet, don't guess—weigh 10 pounds of fertilizer and put it in your spreader. Set the dial on the recommended setting for the spreader to deliver 10 pounds per 1,000 square feet, and see if the amount covers the measured area. If the setting is off, correct it. I have yet to see a spreader that is accurately used by the trusting homeowner, because all of us walk at different speeds and the fertilizers have different sizes of particles. Such checking of calibration is worth both your time and the small expense of wasted fertilizer, for the results of an improperly set spreader can be ruinous to a lawn.

It's now the end of April, and you're all set to feed your grass; but hold off a little longer. The lilacs are almost in bloom. The first week in May is really the time to purchase plant food, and the reasons why, how much, and what kind will be given in the next chapter. As for April, that's all we do. Well, not quite. Some mild evening, when you aren't watching a senseless TV program, go outside and listen. Listen carefully and you might hear the beautiful, haunting cry of the wild geese as they wing northward. If you have any small children, and if they're awake, take them outside to listen to the wonderful sound of spring's promise.

# May and June

AN OLD beat-up dictionary of mine defines grass as "the green covering of the fields." The green covering is vanishing, though, as communities expand and highways eat up the land. Perhaps this is why so much attention is given to preserving our parks and forests and to such associated problems as halting pollution of lakes and rivers and stopping land-development projects that are unnecessarily wiping out wildlife. The wild herds of buffalo are gone; the wolf and grizzly are vanishing; and the coyote, the lonesome troubadour of the prairies, is also disappearing, with no thanks to the courageous airplane hunter. The natural prairies are disappearing. And so are the vacant lots and secret wooded places where little boys once played, coming home to their mothers contentedly tired and dirty and hungry. Years ago there was sure to be some mysterious place nearby where there was something exciting to do. A wonderful tomorrow was just a good night's sleep away. Now we have fenced-off playgrounds and polluted streams. The fields and woods and swimming holes have been replaced by private hunting or fishing clubs and membership swimming pools. In the new housing developments, most of the trees have just been planted, and by the time they grow tall, the youth of the neighborhood will be gone. There will be no nearby place to sit and dream, to use a jackknife for whittling or to carve a willow whistle. The children of this decade, like their grandfathers before them, have dreams that only nature can fulfill and longings that only nature can answer, but, sadly, there are no more outdoor schoolrooms. Unfortunately, man has to destroy too much before he realizes his mistake, and then, just as ardently as he set about destroying, he turns around and tries to put things right.

# All About Fertilizers

Grasses, like animals, require food, air, and water. Unlike animals, however, plants cannot move, so their immediate environment must be the supplier for their existence. The annual cost of lawn maintenance runs into millions of dollars, and most of this is spent for fertilizing grass and eradicating weeds.

## Types of Fertilizer

The types of fertilizer for the general market are natural organic, synthetic organic, and inorganic, in both solid and liquid forms.

The **natural organic fertilizers,** such as sludge and manure, contain carbon. They are semislow-nitrogen-releasing and nonburning fertilizers which, because of their nitrogen content, emit an odor as they break down. This organic nitrogen must be released by soil organisms before it becomes available to the plant, since the nitrogen is not immediately soluble in water. In addition to the nitrogen, organics contain a low percentage of phosphorus and a little "natural" potassium.

The **synthetic organic fertilizers,** of which man-made urea formaldehyde is one, are the slowest nitrogen releasers of all the types regularly used. They contain a high percentage of nitrogen.

**Inorganic fertilizers** generally are the cheapest and the most commonly used. They are quick-acting, and their salts are readily soluble in water. Usually they are sold as complete blends, which means they contain the three nutrients needed by the grass plant: nitrogen, phosphorus, and potassium (referred to as potash). They must always be watered after application.

Disregard the old belief that to the plant there is a difference between organic and inorganic fertilizer. There is none. The grass plant takes most nitrogen in the same form, as a nitrate. The only difference is in the length of time before the nitrogen from an organic or inorganic source is available for use by the plant.

The **liquid fertilizers** are supplementary, "shot in the arm" feeders whose effect is not long-lasting. In general, they consist of one or more inorganic salts or urea (a nitrogenous compound) dissolved in water, and you pay a great price for a little fertilizer and a lot of water. The nutrients in liquid fertilizers can be absorbed by the leaf, but this is not always desirable. I have observed many lawns, especially Merion, fail within a year due to the sole use of liquid fertilizers. You should think twice about applying liquid fertilizers, whether you do it yourself or hire a lawn-service company. There's one time when you're justified in using them: when you are planning a lawn party in a few days and want a quick show of green to impress your guests. A harmless grass dye will accomplish the same purpose, though. I do not recommend liquid fertilizers for lawns and will not speak of them further. Let's go on to plant nutrients.

The three big athletes in golf in recent years have been Nicklaus, Palmer, and Player. The three big elements in fertilizer have the same initials: they are nitrogen, phosphorus, and potassium. These are the necessary elements, of course, but fertilizer advertising continually misleads the public by overemphasizing the importance of trace elements for successful grass growth. **Trace elements,** such as iron, copper, sulfur, manganese, zinc, boron, calcium, and molybdenum, are very rarely needed on a home lawn unless you build it on basement or very poor soil. And in these instances, you're going to need more than trace elements to help you. Always keep in mind that nitrogen, phosphorus, and potassium are the necessary additives and that most soils contain enough of the other plant-food elements. If there is something drastically wrong with your soil, have soil tests taken. In any case, one shot of trace elements will last almost indefinitely; but apply them, as the U.S. Department of Agriculture advises, only if they are recommended by your county agricultural agent or your state agriculture experiment station.

## Choice of Fertilizer and When to Use It

Now that you have learned a little about fertilizer and how the several types work, I can recommend my choice of fertilizer for your lawn. But before doing that, I want to explain why I have chosen the first week in May rather than April, March, or even February for the initial application of plant food to the lawn.

All plant life is influenced by temperature and by the total light received every hour, every day, throughout the year. The "awakening" of grass in the spring and its "going to sleep" in the winter are regulated by a biological clock. With this in mind, you'll agree that the days of March and April are still short, the nights on the long side, and the temperatures low. Oh, the grass is green, all right, but it still isn't growing much. Mother Nature doesn't leap out of bed when the ground is still cold; nor does your grass.

What happens when you apply plant food during this period? Leaching, rotting, and flooding are what happens. Temperatures fluctuate. Melting snow and cold rains wash the fertilizer you paid good money for into low spots where, concentrated, it burns and encourages disease when temperatures rise. Some of the flooded fertilizer is washed away completely, and a lot of leaching into subsurface soil occurs at this time. Much of your plant food ends up flowing over the sidewalk and into the sewer system. Now and then a rise in temperature will break down the remaining fertilizer and cause what can be called an exhilaration of the plant. What this does is stimulate the leaves, making them soft and lush and susceptible to leaf spot and damage by traffic—all told, a weak grass for the tough summer just ahead—because the roots this early are not ready to grow in the cold soil, and you're only getting weak top growth. If there is any growth below, it is hollow and thin and does nothing for the underground root stalks. Meanwhile, your fresh fertilizer is making the early weeds grow stronger and more abundant. Dear homeowner, when does your lawn look its best? When do you mow the most? In the spring, of course. So why stimulate the grass further when it is the most aggressive? And have you forgotten that you applied fertilizer last fall and that the spring growth is very much influenced by this application? Why waste it? Feed your turf just before it is exhausted from that first surge, when it requires food and tonic for the long, long summer ahead. Feed it now, the first week in May, or anytime before the middle of the month.

The *Farmer's Almanac* at one time originated its forecasts of weather conditions from a small plot of land in New England, using degrees and zones as it extended its forecasts around the United States. We will use Chicago as home base for recommending when to fertilize, adding or subtracting two weeks or so as we move to the extreme northern states and western Canada and then toward the milder southern states.

I am basing my recommendations for choice of fertilizer on the premise that your lawn is established Kentucky bluegrass. The exact choice and type of fertilizer for southern grasses can, as mentioned earlier, be obtained by phoning the county agricultural agent at the local office of the Department of Agriculture, which is listed in the telephone book under United States Government, or by writing to the agricultural department of the state university. The best bet, of course, is the most qualified professional turfman in your area, who is always the golf-course superintendent.

Bermuda-grass lawns use large amounts of nitrogen and should be fertilized whenever a slight loss in color is observed. In spring and fall they should have a complete fertilizer, that is, one containing nitrogen, phosphorus, and potassium. After that, nitrogen alone is generally adequate. Bermuda should have a minimum of four applications of fertilizer a year; for superior lawns, apply a couple more times during the growing season.

Here are my recommendations for predominantly bluegrass lawns that stand *two inches or higher* and for other upright rhizome grasses. My choice for established Merion bluegrass lawns—a grass which likes a large amount of nitrogen—is a complete fertilizer with a 2-1-1 ratio, such as 20 percent nitrogen, 10 percent phosphorus, and 10 percent potassium. An ideal combination would be a 16-8-8 makeup (16% N, 8% P, 8% K, 68% bulking material) applied the first week in May (1 pound actual nitrogen, which would be approximately 6 pounds per 1,000 square feet), and again between Labor Day and the first of October, but this time at a double rate: 2 pounds actual nitrogen per 1,000 square feet. There is no need to change calibration on the spreader; just apply in the opposite direction. On or about the first day of summer, June 21, apply a synthetic organic fertilizer (1 pound actual nitrogen per 1,000 square feet). Right here is where we avoid confusion: to figure pounds of "actual nitrogen," take the percentage of total nitrogen, which is always stated on the label, and multiply it by the weight of the fertilizer. For example, with 100 pounds of fertilizer containing 10 percent nitrogen, multiply 0.10 by 100; you get 10 pounds of actual nitrogen, enough for 10,000 square feet. So, if you apply 10 pounds of material, you are applying 1 pound of actual nitrogen per 1,000 square feet.

For the other established bluegrass lawns, make two applications of a complete fertilizer. My choice is 10-10-10. One application now, in May (1 pound actual nitrogen, which would be 10 pounds per 1,000 square feet), and another between Labor Day and October 1 (double rate). However, if your lawn is weak because of inferior maintenance, or if your soil is very sandy, give it another shot on the first day of summer, using a natural organic at the same rate (1 pound actual nitrogen). Or give it an application of a synthetic organic—a urea-formaldehyde fertilizer. I do not recommend anything during this period that could possibly burn a lawn. Too many lawns have burned out because the inorganic fertilizer does not get watered in.

Keep in mind that I haven't recommended fertilizers mixed with insecticides or with weed killers, or "one shot a year" fertilizers. Fertilizers varying slightly in components from 10-10-10 and 16-8-8, such as 12-4-8, 10-3-7, 18-4-6, and 12-4-4, are excellent types. I advise you never to apply your "hot fertilizer" after a rain or when there's dew on the ground, but only on dry grass, and then water in. When fertilizer sticks to a grass blade, it draws moisture from the plant like a poultice. Inorganic fertilizers contain salts, and these salts always collect moisture. Once this action starts, water is drawn from plant tissue and burning results. So water in, please, and be sure to get the fertilizer off the leaf blade and into the soil.

Particle size is important, and I suggest that you always purchase pelleted fertilizer. Although it's more expensive, it's much more convenient to use than the dust or powdered types. These pelleted fertilizers will distribute equally and will not cake. Their main advantage is that they fall or roll off the grass plant, thus minimizing the danger of excessive burn.

My recommended rate of application for feeding a lawn each time is 1 pound of actual nitrogen per 1,000 square feet, and 2 pounds in the fall if you're in a cool-season region. Now you're ready to purchase your fertilizer and feed your lawn. Good luck!

## Mowing—Safely

Grass starts to grow lustily during the month of May and continues to do so until about July, at which time it slackens considerably until fall. Then it revives, but never to resume the vigorous growth of spring and early summer. So now, when you are mowing at least twice a week, you can use some hints on mower safety.

Fill all holes in your lawn for safer cutting and to lessen the chance of sprained ankles and falls. Pick up all toys and stones and sticks before starting to mow, and remember to keep the children at a safe distance, preferably indoors. The best place to check the mechanical functioning of your mower is on bare ground or sidewalk, because leaking gas and oil can kill the grass. If you are using a rotary mower, make sure the blade is good and tight. Put out your cigarette, and be sure the engine and blade have completely stopped. Before taking the gas cap off and filling the tank, wipe away all leaves adhering to the top of the tank and cap. This will prevent leaves or any other foreign matter from getting into and plugging the gas tank. Never overfill a gas tank, because gas may come through a half-tightened cap or air hole and spill on the grass.

Learn the mower controls thoroughly, especially on a new mower. Don't go out there and run over something because you forgot what controls what. Never refuel a hot engine. And don't use an electric mower while the grass is wet. While mowing, stay away from the discharge side of a mower. Stop the engine before going across roads, driveways, and walks, or whenever you leave the mower—even for a moment. Mow steep slopes from side to side, not up and down. Use extreme care with riding mowers on steep inclines. Sharp turns should be avoided, not only because they are hard on the grass, but because you could slip and injure yourself. Practice for awhile with a new machine, remembering that the controls are different from those on your old one. A heavier unit could affect the pivot of your turn, perhaps even causing the mower to slip out of your hands and go chugging down the street. I've seen this happen.

The Outdoor Power Equipment Institute, with the blessings of the U.S. Department of Health, Education, and Welfare and the National Safety Council, is waging an all-out campaign to prevent power-mower accidents. Look for the triangular safety seal on the next mower you buy to make sure that the factory at least has done its part. However, despite all manufacturers' safeguards, a power mower is only as safe as the operator. Keeping that in mind, never allow children under fourteen to handle power mowers. Most mower accidents and many deaths have resulted from something as stupid as the following two examples. A neighbor of mine proudly watched his valiant five-year old son pushing an unwieldly mower The boy got a hernia. In another case, the twelve-year-old son of an exceptionally athletic father got his toes chopped off by a rotary mower. Because his father wouldn't tolerate a "sissy," the boy had to grapple with a machine beyond his ability—and he lost. Most boys of fourteen years and over have the strength and stature, however, to handle small machines—provided proper instruction has been given by some capable adult.

## Getting Back at Weeds

Next on our maintenance program comes weeds. These outlaws usually invade weakened lawns, which probably have become that way as a result of irresponsibility and poor maintenance by the homeowner. But the best way out of a difficuty is through it. . . .

## Causes of Weed Infestation

The absolutely avoidable practices that always result in a poor lawn are too little fertilization, improper watering, and improper mowing. I'll give you an example. Nearby, an expensive housing development, five blocks long and five years old, has just been completed. The developer took his time and each year built only one block of homes, and as each block was completed he put in a Merion lawn. There are five blocks of sodded Merion lawns. Beautiful? Classic looking? Not quite. If you started walking at the block sodded in the first year, you would see that the lawns are all weeds. The second block is the same, and in both blocks a few homeowners are already resodding. The third-year block is a little better, but you can see definite signs of deterioration. The fourth block looks good, and the one just completed is beautiful, but it won't be for long.

What happened? Neglect. The homeowners forgot to fertilize, or they used poor products or didn't apply enough, or they used too much and caused burning and disease. I suspect they thought beautiful grass like this was going to take care of itself. They mowed it too short, both infrequently and with a dull mower that chewed instead of cut. Worst of all, the homeowners encouraged this ghetto of weeds by the intolerable practice of light daily sprinklings. Like their fathers before them, who sat every evening with their hoses, conversing, smoking, and downing a beer or two, these homeowners have babied their lawns with hand watering or sprinklers for a brief period each evening. This destructive practice hasn't changed in thirty years.

I want also to clear-up, once for all, the common yet false notion that nearly every homeowner seems to have: that he got his weeds from his next-door neighbor. Sorry, but this is seldom so. Weeds are carried by wind, foot traffic, and birds, and you will always have them. Weed seeds are also in the soil, of course, and the seeds may remain there for years before germinating. If you carry out a good maintenance program, though, you'll never have to worry about and infestation of weeds. The few that will come your way can be pulled out by hand. Why waste money, time, and effort to eliminate only a few, and perhaps have an accident with your chemicals? Let the children go out and weed with jackknives or simple hand weeding tools. Give them shopping bags, and a bonus for the fellow who digs out the most with the biggest root systems. (But get the roots out! This is important.) Then call it a tie and give them all a prize. The best midriff reducer I know is pulling weeds. With the blessings of all doctors, I strongly recommend this for the housewife. Put on a pair of loose slacks and give it a try. You'll lose a few pounds, and if you're the nervous type—and who isn't nowadays?—you'll sleep a lot better that night.

## Types of Weeds and Ways to Control Them

There are three types of weeds: broad-leaved, small-leaved, and narrow grasslike weeds. Most books on lawns list only broad-leaved and grassy weeds, classifying the small-leaved weeds with the broad-leaved. I have found that the best control is to use a selective weed killer against a particular weed. If both small-leaved and broad-leaved weeds are present, then a mixture of two selective weed killers is the most effective. Happily, the small- and broad-leaved weeds can be easily eradicated, but the grassy weeds are a different matter. Some of them, like quack grass, which is also called couch grass, (perhaps its only other polite name), are impossible to eradicate with weed killers unless you also wish to get rid of your desirable grasses.

Of the three weed categories, I'll name only the weeds that commonly plague the homeowner. More important, I'll identify each weed by category. It's my purpose to name the numerous chemicals for eradicating the lawn outlaws. Some are very good, some only fair. Read the label instructions carefully. You're reading information that has cost a fortune to obtain, and it was all spent in your favor. The effectiveness and safety of any weed killers, or of any pesticide, are of greater importance than convenience, easy application, or low cost.

Among the **broad-leaved weeds** commonly found throughout

North America are dandelion, plantain, ground ivy (creeping charlie), sheep sorrel, purslane, and wild geranium. All these common weeds can be controlled by 2,4-D, which does not harm the grass. This is the most spectacular weed killer discovered, for it eradicates the outstanding outlaw in your lawn, the broad-leaved weed. A small-leaved weed, such as clover or chickweed, is never as noticeable as, say, a dandelion patch. A hormone-type weed killer that kills by overstimulation, 2,4-D is absorbed by the leaves and carried through the plant's vascular system. The result is twisted and curled leaves.

Some of the well-known **small-leaved weeds** are clover, chickweed (common and mouse-ear), knotweed, yarrow, spotted spurge, oxalis, and henbit. A good control for them is 2,4,5-TP (Silvex).

The weed killers named above should be applied when the temperature is over 50 degrees and the day sunny, with no prediction of rain for at least a day, and preferably over a soil with adequate moisture content. Do this about a week or two after fertilizing so the grass can grow in and form a tight sod over the bare spots left by the dead weeds. Applying a fertilizer at the same time, unless it's a nonburning variety, results in a double shock for the plant. A more important reason for applying fertilizers and weed killers at different times, however, is that most fertilizers have to be washed off the plant, whereas weed killers for broad-leaved and small-leaved weeds must be left on the blades of grass, which should not be mowed for at least a few days. The same principle applies to fertilizer and insecticide mixtures, although here watering might be permissible since some insects are killed by the soaking of insecticides into the soil. I have never found the application of "one shot" packages to be as effective as separate applications. Besides, you're sometimes paying for weed killer or insecticide that you don't need.

Herbicides should be applied in the spring when the weeds are young and lush and growing rapidly, rather than later when they have put down hardened, deep root stems. Most chemicals shock grass to some extent when they are applied, a fact that should be kept in mind no matter what the advertisements urge. In springtime, grass growth is vigorous and in its most recuperative stage, thus best able to recover from an overdose. As a final precaution, the chemicals should never be applied during a wind because their contact can be dangerous to shrubs, flowers, and other ornamental plants. Not only can it cause bad feelings between you and your neighbors, but it might make you eligible for a lawsuit, or require you to pay the cost of replacing plants (both yours and your neighbor's), or, worst of all, make you lie!

Let me tell you about an experience some time ago when I wanted to eradicate the many weeds in my common Kentucky bluegrass lawn, which was one year old. Being very busy both night and day during the golf season, as are all golf-course superintendents, I decided to borrow an ancient 200-gallon fairway sprayer rig and spray my lawn. Picture now a very old tractor, painted red and blue, hauling a monstrosity, also red and blue, down the highway at ten miles an hour, wobbling as it went. On the golf course no one would look twice at such machinery, but on the highway it had an antic, disreputable appearance, especially with me perched on top under a battered straw hat. Barney Oldfield at the wheel! The motorists seemed quite unsettled at the sight and clearly regarded me and my rig as a catastrophe looking for a place to happen. And so we were, as it turned out, though I was actually unaware of this as at last I reached home and made a few strategic sprays in the back and front yards. The wind was blowing toward the north.

A week later, my neighbor's geraniums and roses began to wilt and die. I immediately realized what had happened and went to work concealing the true cause. I told my friend (forgive me, Heinie!) that a great flower disease, an epidemic never before seen, had struck our neighborhood and was devastating flowers everywhere. I even apologized for not having warned him to take precautions, as I'd done with the other nearby neighbors. They, I said, naturally had applied a preventive chemical when they first heard of the epidemic's arrival from Morocco. Well, I don't think my old friend believed me in the first place, and he certainly didn't after he questioned my neighbor to the south, who reportedly replied, "What disease? Morocco? Come in out of the sun and have a beer. Say, did you see what that nut next door was driving last week?" No, never lie to your neighbors.

The leaves of **grasslike weeds** are long and narrow, similar to those of desirable grasses, but are frequently wider and much coarser. The most familiar annual weed in this category is CRABGRASS.

Although there are chemicals to kill it, it is still the most difficult to control. One reason is that each crabgrass plant produces thousands of seeds. In cool climates, the plant comes up in late spring, but in the South it usually appears earlier, when the soil first warms to about 60° F. Crabgrass is both unwelcome and sly. It doesn't come up all at once, but sprouts throughout a prolonged hot summer, when conditions are conducive to its germination. As crabgrass emerges it resembles a fat spear, apple green in color. Then two clawlike spears appear, and finally comes the crab appearance for which it is named. The weed's flat stems spread out fast; lying low, they are difficult to cut. The weed is hard to destroy after it has gotten started because chemicals have to be sprayed frequently for full control. It is better to wait until autumn or, even better, the following spring, and then apply preemergence crabgrass killer. Besides, some postemergence chemicals that are applied to crabgrass are tough on Merion. Live with it until fall, cutting the grass high. Since crabgrass is affected by shade, the best deterrence is in getting lawn grass to grow higher and denser than the weed. Infrequent watering helps to discourage additional sprouting. At the first frost, crabgrass will turn reddish brown, then whitewashed brown. It will stand out like a sore thumb, and you will realize how much or how little of this nuisance you have. If you are attempting to grow a zoysia lawn in the northern states, remember that zoysia also turns reddish brown at the first frost. So don't confuse a zoysia lawn with a lawn that has been taken over completely by crabgrass.

The best crabgrass killer for fall is a chemical that comes in pellet form, calcium arsenate. (It also controls grubworms.) Apply as directed. I have found that a follow-up application of calcium arsenate the following spring will be effective for several years. For springtime application only, the crabgrass killer I prefer above all others is Dacthal, because it's very effective, safe to use, and does no harm to the desired turf. Its only disadvantage is the cost each spring, since it leaves no residue and so isn't available for the next year; but it's worth every cent. Apply it in the spring before the crabgrass germinates. Apply it for two springs, then skip the third one. If you have followed our maintenance program, your sod should by then be healthy enough without a crabgrass killer. For homeowners who have followed an excellent maintenance program, and who don't like to use chemicals but still wish to control their crabgrass, especially in the transition zones where crabgrass flourishes best, I recommend the planting of shade trees or a ground cover, other than grass, that does well in your area. Crabgrass loves sunlight and can't stand shade. I realize this is an expensive alternative, but it's one that works all the time—forever.

Another grassy weed is annual bluegrass, more commonly called POA ANNUA. *Poa* in the established turf is the golf-course superintendent's worst foe, and it's becoming a nuisance in the homeowner's lawn as he seeks to cut his lawn lower and lower and to water more and more. Its prominence is a direct result of this type of maintenance. In certain parts of Canada and some of the states, *Poa* is classified as a serious turf weed. In most of the country it is still called a grass. In appearance it is similar to Kentucky bluegrass; actually, it is the black sheep of the bluegrass family. *Poa* is therefore difficult to distinguish from Kentucky bluegrass when it is growing vigorously in the spring and fall. In the extreme northern United States and in most of Canada it does quite well and is rarely recognized in the home lawn. At places like Jasper National Park and Banff Springs Golf Course it makes a luxurious putting turf on the greens; fairways 14, 15, and 16 at Jasper, which are surrounded by a lake, have the finest turf I have seen anywhere, and all *Poa!* But harsh Canadian winters are tough on *Poa,* and it takes a long time to come back each spring. In other areas—and it's common in all states—it is much more of a pest. But it has a very limited ability to adapt itself to extreme conditions, like hot humid summers, harsh winters, and dry spells. One reason *Poa* is such a sissy is that it has shallow roots. During the stress periods of summer, it wilts and dries in patches, turning yellow and coarse. *Poa* reseeds itself constantly, at varying rates depending on how cool the summer is, growing most profusely in the spring. At this heavy seeding, the white seed heads are coarse and hard to cut, and they make the grass look white. Although *Poa* is classified an annual, it sometimes survives through hot summers and mild winters; in extreme cases it survives three or more years. Almost any chemicals you use to combat other lawn problems will hinder this grass weakling. One way to control it is to use calcium arsenate in the fall. Recently some selective chemicals have been perfected for the eradication and control of *Poa annua,* and more are coming out. The college of agriculture at your state university can give you the name of the most recent one.

For perennial grass weeds, like QUACK GRASS, there is no easy control. They can be eliminated by careful spot treatment with a powerful chemical called Dalapon, or by sterilizing the soil, which is costly. One safeguard is to make sure that the soil you buy is free of these weeds or has been treated for them. When scientists discover a grass for lawns with a root system and growth habits like those of quack grass and can combine these with the desirable characteristics of Kentucky bluegrass, we will have no further need of books like this. We then will have the ideal grass.

The only advice I can give you for the other tough grass weeds is one you are well aware of—hand weeding.

Well, that does it for weeds. The chemicals I advised you to use are usually not recommended for the short-cut grasses like Bermuda and bent. St. Augustine is also touchy with some of the weed killers, especially the arsenates. A homeowner should probably have professional help with the first chemical application on these grasses. The way to eradicate broad-leaved and small-leaved weeds completely is to follow up with the same chemical two weeks after the first application.

I have one last word about weeds. There is one time when weeds aren't undesirable at all. That time is when your little boy or girl comes running up with a handful of dandelions and says, "Here—I picked them just for you!" This bouquet will probably be the most beautiful and precious you will ever receive.

## Stamping Out Insects

This is a good time to consider pest control. There are two categories of insects we will worry about: those above the ground and those below. One type chews and feeds on leaves and stems, and the other destroys roots.

## Aboveground Insects

The most common aboveground pests are cutworms, sod webworms (larvae only), and chinch bugs (see pages 19–20).

## Belowground Insects

The belowground insects most devastating to grass are grubs, which are the larvae of the Japanese beetle, the May or June beetle, the Oriental beetle, and various types of chafers. Hatched from eggs laid in the ground by the female beetles, the larvae stay one to three inches below the ground from ten months to three years. The grubs are U- or horseshoe-shaped, whitish in color, and from one-quarter inch to one inch in length. Their feeding on the roots may cause dead whitish or brownish patches, perhaps first brought to your attention by the sudden appearances of crows, blackbirds, and other birds that love these plump delicacies. Moles and skunks also feed on grubs. So getting rid of the grubs will also help indirectly to chase away those *Wind in the Willow* characters. Make a test by gripping some grass and pulling up; if you have many grubs, the grass will come up with no effort. Then scratch the soil a little, and you'll see the grubs for sure.

Some of the other subsurface insects are ants and earthworms. These two don't feed on the grass, of course, but ant colonies and worm casts and mounds are sometimes a nuisance, though they're less bothersome on home lawns than on golf courses, where grass is mowed very short.

## In Defense of Earthworms

There is one creature about which I wish to make it plain where I stand. This is the lowly earthworm. Experts recently have stated that the earthworm is not needed in lawn or garden, that it does not enrich the soil, and that its constant aerification of the soil usually is not beneficial. Get rid of earthworms with chemicals, they say, and for their borings substitute mechanical aerification and wetting agents to let minerals and water into the soil. Well, all I can say is that these statements are made by classroom experts and not by those of us who have grown excellent gardens, flowers, and grass in our yards, and by all of us who (sentimentality definitely enters into this) have dug up earthworms for fishing bait. I have observed that lawns abundant with earthworms rarely have any harmful grubs. I checked this observation with older superintendents who have had longer experience than I've had, and they agree: no prominence of grubs where lots of earthworms are present. I further want to state that I have never seen localized dry spots or fairy rings where these harmless friends of the soil are numerous. Finally, no thatch problem develops with a large population of earthworms. The earthworm castings cover and mix with the thatch on the surface of the soil, hastening the decomposition of dead leaves, stems, and other debris. This is the same way a compost pile is made, except in this case the earthworms do it.

The gardens I've examined have always seemed to me to bloom more abundantly where earthworms have been present. If you wish any further affidavits, ask the best gardener I know, my mother, who brought her family through many thin times with the help of her wonderful garden. Our garden was packed with earthworms. Not long ago a guest on TV's now defunct "What's My Line?" gave his occupation as raising earthworms for sale through the mails. When a panel member asked him if most of the worms were sold to fishermen, the worm farmer replied, "No, on the contrary, 80 to 90 percent are sold to gardeners to enrich the soil."

There is one more thing to say on behalf of earthworms. Robins and thrushes and other ground-feeding birds live on them. I would rather have earthworms, with all their harmless mounds and castings, than miss the delightful sight of even one robin straining to pull out a meal.

## Insecticides

The harmful insects above and below the ground in your yard may be controlled by many excellent chemicals, of which I consider chlordane the best. I prefer the 40–50 percent wettable powders to the liquid chlordane, which is an emulsified concentrate harsh to such grass as bent and the fine fescues when not applied correctly.

Be attentive now, because this point is important. For the aboveground pests, the lawn should be well watered before you apply a chemical. Then the insecticide, to which one ounce of biodegradable household detergent is added per gallon of mix, should be sprayed over the lawn. This covers better than the undiluted compound. Don't mow or water the grass for a few days. Spray again in a few weeks, because, no matter how careful you are, the effect of aboveground control is soon lost as untreated leaves grow up; and of course it sometimes rains after your first application. There is also the necessity to water and mow your grass, so some of the chemical is always wasted.

The materials used against belowground insects must be placed on the surface and watered in to be effective. Of course, if you get invaded by both above- and belowground insects, follow both recommended procedures. First, for aboveground insects, don't water; wait two or three days, then soak the chemical in. You'll get both types this way.

The responsible homeowner should keep all lawn and garden chemicals in a cabinet, in the same way he keeps medicines safe in a medicine cabinet. If you have small children, I suggest you put a lock on the cabinet or place the chemicals on a high shelf out of reach. The accidental poisoning of children and pets most often results from careless storage or thoughtless disposal of pesticides. The United States Department of Agriculture requires that the words "Caution," "Warning," or "Poison" be given a prominent place on labels; but remember, the majority of children who are poisoned can't read. Be especially careful never to place liquid pesticides in a soft-drink container, as you might be tempted to do if you sometimes borrow a small amount from your neighbor. Most liquid pesticides look like root beer in color and are a natural come-on for kids. Every homeowner should have the phone number of a poison-control center handy in case of possible emergency. Dispose of any lawn or garden pesticides that have a missing or unreadable label. It's better to duplicate the cost of the contents than to risk the consequences of putting something on your lawn that you aren't sure of. Worse yet, it could be swallowed. To prescribe an antidote, the doctor must know immediately the exact composition of a poison. So throw chemicals away without hesitation if labels are unreadable. One last precaution: wash the spraying equipment after each use, mixing a little household detergent with the water and rinsing several times.

## Rachel Carson, Bless Her

A lot of discussion and some alarm have centered recently on pesticides and other chemicals. More than anything else, Rachel Carson's *Silent Spring* has informed the public that careless use of insecticides has a deadly effect upon wildlife—actually, on all life. This book divided the public into two camps. One group blasted the book for unnecessarily alarming the public; at the same time, it extolled the wonderful benefits of pesticides. The second group was all for outlawing many chemicals and placing restrictions on others. In a way, both were right and both were wrong. But she made people think, and her crusade sparked a useful examination of the composition and use of chemicals. I believe Miss Carson wanted manufacturers to take more care in labeling and distributing the pesticides, and users to exercise more respect and care when applying these poisons. She accomplished this objective very well.

However, I would like to bring out a few facts, and if I seem to get on a soapbox—well, that's my intention. Fifty times more deaths are caused by medicines than by pesticides. The misuse of aspirin alone causes more deaths each year than all pesticide cases combined. Yet how can we argue against the use of pesticides when it has been demonstrated that by controlling mosquitoes with DDT we have practically eliminated malaria and sleeping sickness, thereby saving countless lives every year? There are many other examples of the beneficial effects of these chemicals. On the other hand, consider this thought: to get a simple chemical from a drugstore, you need a doctor's prescription; and yet readily available to anyone are chemicals that can wipe out whole neighborhoods! The difference, of course, is that one is for human beings, the other for plants. You might think that no one in his right mind would buy a dangerous chemical and dump it into water the public will drink.

Yet this is exactly what is being done. What do you think happens when industries and communities dump their chemical wastes and assortments of sewage into streams and lakes?

Rachel Carson was making an eloquent plea to all of us who disturb nature's fine balance with attempts at conquest, instead of cooperation. Who among us would wish to endanger the health of the people, or to wipe out forever the fireflies and destroy the harmless dragonfly and songbird with misuse of chemicals? We must remember to work with nature, not against her.

## Seeding and Sodding

You've been patient so far about not seeding your lawn, even though your neighbors are doing it, so the next order of business is to answer two questions: Is it better to seed in the spring or fall? And which is better, seeding or sodding?

### Spring or Fall Seeding?

I advise seeding in the fall instead of in the spring because soil temperatures are more favorable in the fall. Spring weather is too unpredictable. So is spring fever. Days of snow, wet soil, and cold harsh winds are mixed with intermittent days of beautifully mild weather, and the latter tease the homeowner into getting started outdoors. Certainly a grass lawn can be planted at this time, and many are, especially in western Canada, the Northwest Territories, and Alaska, where the summers are short and end quickly after a brief growing season. Keep in mind that all living things—including you and me—emerge only after incubation at a uniform temperature. For grass, this means warm soil and consecutive warm days for maximum germination of seed planted.

The seed companies' instructions allow plenty of time for the seed to germinate. For example, common Kentucky bluegrass is described as taking twenty-one days for germination. Don't waste your time and effort getting the seed started in the spring. You may lose everything to flooding, rot, or a fungus called damping-off, which too often kills young seedlings at this time. Why take a chance when you can cut that germination period in half by planting in the moist, warm ground of late summer and early fall? Take a hint from nature: that's the time when seeds are dropped.

Another advantage of seeding lawns in the late summer or early fall is that weeds spring up more rapidly and profusely in spring and vigorously compete with the seedlings. And you can bet that weeds are better able to get through the hot summer, which is the season now facing your young lawn. This leaves you with only one way to save your lawn, hand weeding. Spraying with weed killer during this time would also endanger the young grass. But if you have seeded in the spring, wait to spray until after August 15, when the grass is more mature.

In the South the situation is entirely different. It's self-evident that warm-region grasses which go dormant in the winter must be planted in the spring. Cool-region grasses, however, are seeded in the fall; otherwise in the spring the cool-region grasses would have to face the perils of dust, dry winds, extreme heat.

Finally, grass takes less time to develop into mature sod when it's planted in the fall than it does when it's planted in the spring. In my own experience, a homeowner needs three years to develop satisfactory sod from seed. The first year yields about 20 percent coverage, because the grass grows straight up. Second-year coverage will be about 70 percent, because then the grass starts to spread out and fill in. During the third year the final 10 percent grows and forms a solid, dense turf. However, if the grass is planted in the late summer or fall, it will make a dense turf in two years. The reason is the good growth during those ideal warm days of fall; that is, the growth produced from late summer to winter is comparable to that achieved during the long months from spring germination to winter. The late start is compensated for by conditions that are more favorable. The sod nurseries, interested in sales, take this shortcut because it's to their profit to produce in the shortest time possible. Why don't you? If you want to read more about the seeding procedure, see page 75.

## Sodding

If you have bought or will buy a new home during the spring, why not consider sodding your lawn, especially if you have terraced slopes and banks where erosion can be a problem? Sodding costs more initially, but it offers many advantages. First, it can be done any time, though spring is best for southern grasses. Its beauty is immediately available to you and your neighbors. Second, since it's weed-free, there is no time or expense wasted in spraying for weeds, no danger of chemical burn. Third, flooding will not wash it out, nor will high winds blow it away, leaving you with the expense of starting all over again. Fourth, there is less danger of fungus attack. The best and last point is the sodded lawn's readiness for traffic in less than two weeks. Keep in mind that the recently purchased sod usually hasn't quite completed its growth cycle, and this is actually to your benefit. It completes the maturity cycle in your lawn, sending down eager white roots to make contact with the soil of your sod bed and knit the pieces together—providing, of course, that correct maintenance procedures have been followed.

If you add all these advantages you'll find that in the long run a sodded lawn will cost you less or certainly no more than a seeded lawn. There is one disadvantage to sodding, which may make seeding preferable, even if it does take longer; but this will be discussed on page 79. Now, back to sodding.

A lawn should have a minimum of four inches of good soil so the roots of the newly laid sod can grow down into a desirable medium. If there is only a thin layer of dirt, the grass roots grow down through this skimpy layer, reach impenetrable hard clay, and stop. From here on, your chances of having a desirable lawn are very slim. Most of the sod sold is grown on peat loam, which germinates fast and is easy to load, unload, and lay. But peat sod placed on a thin surface of good dirt or over clay-loam topsoil will shrink and dry out unless it's carefully watered and watched. Sometimes the sodded lawn may look good for a long time, especially if the weather is favorable and you follow all the instructions. But with the arrival of the first spell of hot, humid weather, your lawn will start to have trouble. The roots are unable to burrow through the "concrete" layer. The result is poor color, weed infestation, and thinning out.

This also results, I believe, in localized dry spots and fairy rings, especially on Merion bluegrass.

What should a homeowner do? Well, most nurseries have some sod grown in firmer bases than peat loam to please people like me who sometimes *insist* on a heavy sod. You can do the same. However, it's easier and much more important to have at least four inches of desirable topsoil spread over the subgrade in your sod bed. Just remember there is no such thing as cheap black dirt.

More and more building contractors are now doing the sodding as they complete their homes, so that the buyer gets the lawn with the house. This is an attractive selling point, but of course you're paying for it. Many of these lawns are done with great care, and you're getting your money's worth. Nevertheless, the home builder should stick with what he knows best, building, and the homeowner should check his contract and insist on getting what he's entitled to. Don't put up with a roughly graded lawn on which an inch or two (if you're lucky) of good soil is spread and quickly sodded. If this is going to happen, it's better to hire a qualified landscaper instead (get three bids) and have him do the job properly.

Sodding is good exercise and isn't hard to do, provided you have prepared a proper bed (see page 75). It's somewhat like laying a tile floor, except you want to stagger the ends of each of the sod strips. (If you're confused, look at a brick wall to see how the bricks are staggered.) Start out by laying a straight line of sod down the middle of your yard. Now, sod on one side and then on the other. If you have help, one team can work on one side and a second team on the other side of the center line. Rake out the footprints as you go along, closely snugging or butting the pieces and remembering to stagger the ends so they'll knit better. If the ends form straight lines and you get a flooding rain, the lines open into channels and cause erosion between the strips; sometimes the strips move around, especially on slopes and banks. When laying sod on any prominent incline, be sure to place your sod strips (usually eighteen inches wide by six feet long) across the face of the slope and not up and down. Just before sodding, try to watch a job being done by professionals. This will prove more instructive than anything I can say.

After sodding has been completed, roll the lawn a few times;

then really water it. I mean *soak* it. Give it so much water that when you lift a corner of sod it's dripping wet and the soil underneath is muddy. Make this test in many places, especially at borders, like the sidewalks, where the sod strips first dry out. Now that you think you've soaked it enough, water it again, this time using some boards to walk on so you don't sink in. After a few days, when the sod is firm again, fertilize it with natural organic matter. From now on, play it by ear, rolling and watering about twice a week until the sod has knitted and made sufficient contact with the soil underneath so that, when you gently try to lift up a strip, you can't dislodge it.

Why use organic fertilizer and not something more concentrated? Well, spreading excessive amounts of a fertilizer with a high nitrogen content over a newly sodded lawn stimulates a lush top growth but does little for the shocked root system below. Such a superficially strong lawn will lull a homeowner into relaxing, only to give him trouble later in adverse weather. So go easy the first year with excessive surface fertilization. Wait until next year, when the roots will have made a comeback and penetrated deep into the soil. Besides, if you follow the instructions on page 76, an application of fertilizer will already have been mixed into the soil bed.

There are a few other things to keep in mind about sodding. Measure your lawn correctly before purchasing sod. It's better to have a few pieces left over than to be short and have part of the lawn unsodded. Make sure the sod you buy is certified, with a guarantee for so many months. Comply with the instructions, but be sure the sod comes from your locality—you don't want to chase after someone two states away if your sod comes up in weeds. Nor should you take a chance on a sod grown in different soil and climate.

## Vegetative Planting

For you Northerners who aren't familiar with southern grasses, vegetative planting is the means by which a popular southern strain, such as Bermuda, zoysia, or St. Augustine, is propagated—by the replanting of living grass. The methods in use are plugging, sprigging, stolonizing, and strip sodding. Planting has to be done in these ways because the warm-region grasses, like those named above, and most of the bents, cannot be grown from seed. They won't produce a true plant or hybrid.

Plugging is the most economical method of vegetative planting. For the average southern lawn, of 800 to 1,000 square yards, plugging usually is done with a special hand tool. Large lawns and industrial areas can be plugged by machines that place 1 to 1½-inch plugs of grass every 6 inches in rows 8 inches apart. In hand plugging for the home lawn, the plugs can vary from 2 to 3 inches in size and can be spaced further apart; however, the closer the plugs are, the sooner they will fill your lawn.

An individual grass plant is called a sprig. Sprigging is done during spring in straight rows or furrows, as one would find in a vegetable garden, using single sprigs or stolons (runners). If the rows are close together, the lawn will form more quickly. Commercial growers, like sod nurseries, set sprigs in rows about 36 inches apart. When stem growth is long enough, the sprigs bushes are chopped, or shredded, and sold by the sacked bushel as "stolons." Each bushel will stolonize about 100 square feet. Stolonizing works best with finer grasses, such as bents, which have even growth and distribution. But there's a higher mortality rate in the stolonizing of zoysia or Bermuda than by plugging or sprigging.

Strip sodding consists of transplanting lengths of sod, and the grass of the sod will creep across the bare space between the strips. Except for regular sodding, strip sodding is the most expensive method of vegetative planting. For this reason I recommend it only for steep grades in the lawn where erosion is a problem, or for where special terracing effects are desired.

# July and August

DURING THE dog days of July and August, when the humidity and heat get unbearable, dogs and children—in fact, all of us—become lazy and like to take it easy. Grass does, too. It slows down and conserves its energy. The tip-off to this normal, semidormant stage is the grass's change in color. The average homeowner usually doesn't recognize this symptom, so he naturally is distressed when he sees the grass go off color. He then does things to his turf that can do more harm than good. I will endeavor to calm those fears with some common-sense rules for lawn maintenance during the hot summer, but first let's dwell a moment on the current water situation.

The problem of water shortage in several areas of the continental United States arises not from localized conditions of minor drought, but from the fact that water is taken from the earth's veins and used faster than it's returned. Since World War II, industrial expansion has increased the consumption of water ten times—and the water that is returned is contaminated. The homeowner, too, uses more water than ever. Extra bathrooms, swimming pools, automatic watering systems, dishwashers, and automatic washing machines (most of which use six times as much water as the wringer types) all contribute to the problem. Is it any wonder, then, that during the course of every summer we read alarming articles by scientists, engineers, and conservationists about the water shortage? Of course the homeowner is promptly warned to water his lawn only at certain hours—sometimes not at all—under penalty of fine. However, down the street the local car wash continues to flush thousands of gallons of water down the drain, and giant industries keep right on defiling our rivers and streams with their slop, rivers and streams that could help relieve the threat of acute water shortage. This extravagant use and misuse cause the shortage, not nature's sluggishness in replenishing watersheds. With that in mind, let's see how the homeowner can get the most from summer irrigation and still reduce his mounting water bill.

## Proper Watering Practices

Grass flourished long before man began to water it. It did all right, and it will continue to do well if left alone. But we don't want grass a foot high, and the heights we now cultivate demand effort and proper watering practices. My first declaration is that a lawn needn't be watered more than once a week, if it's done properly. Contrary to popular notions, a little every day or every second day only encourages a very short, weak root system, which, during the hot, dry days of summer, will let you down every time. When outdoor temperatures get extremely high, moisture evaporates from the leaf surfaces faster than the roots can replenish it. Plants with adequate root systems become semidormant, conserving their energy until conditions become ideal again for growing. These plants survive. However, when a weak or babied root system becomes semidormant, the turf begins to wilt and die out, sometimes failing completely. In any event, weeds come in as the grass thins out. And when weeds begin to take over a lawn, the homeowner really has troubles. So water infrequently but heavily. *Do not sprinkle* your lawn; put aside the urge. When the grass plants do not get water every day, their roots grope downward to where moisture is available. Of course, after a week or more of parching weather, even the subsoil dries out, and irrigation is necessary—heavy irrigation, so as to soak the subsoil as well as the surface. Then wait another week before watering. You'll be surprised (and delighted) at how often a good rain occurs at the end of this sixth or seventh day.

While on the subject of home irrigation, let's clear up a few more misunderstandings. How may times have you been advised by experts, also advocating heavy watering, to water four to six inches deep? But have you ever been told how you are going to know when you've watered to that depth? Of course not. You'd have to be a worm cruising at minus six inches to know when you're all wet. Some soils are sandy, some are clay, others are good loam. Each absorbs water differently. The best way of determining when the grass has had enough water is to walk on the lawn. When water comes up under your feet—I am not talking about puddled water, but water that squishes as you walk—your lawn has had enough. This is the only way to water your lawn in a dry spell. Don't give it a wish and a promise each evening.

If you are curious to know how much water you are using, make a simple test. Set a one-pound coffee can just a few feet away from the sprinkler and put another one near the end of the spray. Turn on the sprinkler and soak the lawn until it squishes. The height of water in each can will indicate how much water has gone into the soil and how effectively. Variations in the contents of the coffee cans means your sprinkler isn't distributing the water evenly, so you may want to buy a sprinkler that does a proper job.

Remember always to overlap when you irrigate, so that your whole lawn gets watered completely. This is a good argument for automatic watering, if you can afford it. The pop-up valve heads are spaced in the ground so that the whole lawn is watered thoroughly. The valves can be turned on and off automatically by an electric timer. During dry spells, when watering is restricted to certain hours, usually during the night, this system allows the homeowner to get a good night's sleep. It's better than setting an alarm clock and waking up every so often to move the sprinklers. Or persuading the wife to try the joys of nocturnal lawn irrigation.

Of the many kinds of sprinklers, I prefer the oscillating types that slowly spray in a rectangle or square. (Aren't most lawns square?) But any sprinkler that throws water out slowly and gives the water a chance to penetrate the soil is far superior to the ones that whirl a mile a minute. Sprinklers of this type flood everything in a short time, confusing the poor homeowner into thinking the soil has had enough water, when actually the reason the water stands is that it hasn't had time to filter through the hard dry layer of earth. The homeowner, not realizing this, moves the sprinkler after very short intervals. Next day he wonders why his lawn is dry again. So be a little selective when buying a sprinkler for your grass. If you don't like the way it operates, take it back. At a golf course, the sprinklers are chosen for durability and are set to revolve slowly and steadily. You should be equally discriminating. However, if you have already invested in one that rotates rapidly, use it wisely. Move it after an area floods. Then, after the water has had a chance to penetrate the linoleum-like surface, water the same spot again. Likely as not the water will seep in more quickly this time because the surface has been softened.

Now, let's briefly review our facts on watering.

We know from checking our rain gauge how much rain has fallen, so we can determine approximately how long to wait before we water again.

We know how long it takes our lawn to be watered and how much water we are using.

We also know a little more about sprinklers and the importance of overlapping our moves. I would like to mention here that the old idea of watering only in the mornings is a fallacy. Watering is permissible at any time, day or night, provided the rate is slow.

Now that you're anxious to start watering and making your own tests, let me tell you something that will save you lots of time and money: If you live where cool-region rhizome grasses (Kentucky bluegrass strains) are grown satisfactorily, and if you don't mow under two inches, the truth is that you don't have to water in April or May or early June, and in late June you need to water only if very adverse conditions exist. If you live in an area where both cool-region and warm-region grasses are grown, or warm-region grasses alone, then you'll have to water sooner. But if you live in a climate like Chicago's or cooler, spare yourself—and conserve water—for those three months. My fairways are of bent, which is a luxury water grass, and *Poa annua,* a surface grass with very poor resistance to anything and everything; and they are cut very short. If I don't water in May and only begin to do so in June when I can't hold out any longer, why should you, who are growing a bluegrass lawn cut to a height of two inches, water before July? Give your turf a chance to get its roots down deep into the soil. Don't tease it and spoil it and weaken it like an overprotected child by watering before watering is necessary. Keep in mind you'll have lots of rain in this period, and by the time the stress period arrives, your lawn will have developed the strength to pull through. Don't worry; it won't die if it's healthy. It may go dormant, but it won't die. If your lawn is newly seeded or sodded, if it's in poor condition, or if you've burned it with something, then irrigate; otherwise, wait, and plan to start watering just before July 4.

## Applying Chemicals and Fertilizers

During July and August, a homeowner should apply chemicals to his lawn only in cases of severe disease. Even then he should have careful guidance or, better still, employ experts—chosen carefully—with proper equipment. All chemicals shock grass, but in the spring the grass has the ability to recover. Not so during a hot spell. I've seen many lawns damaged or wiped out completely by chemicals applied during the hot, humid days of summer by homeowners or careless lawn-maintenance people who should have known better. It is wiser to wait out this stress period without bothering the lawn.

The same advice applies to fertilizing. No chemical fertilizer should be applied during July and August, no matter where you live—unless the job is done by experts. If it is absolutely necessary to apply a touch of plant food to your lawn during this time, use natural organic fertilizer only, not inorganic (solid or liquid) or synthetics.

These guidelines apply to flowers, too. In any season spray roses only in the morning. However, don't spray them at all, even in the brief cool of the morning, during a hot spell. Wait until the hot spell is broken, or apply only half the recommended dosage. Under the guidance of the most astute experts I've tried many chemicals for roses, and I've found that during a hot spell, any compound that would give satisfactory protection against insects and disease would also scar or burn this most beautiful of blossoms, even if applied in the middle of the night. You'll find more on fertilizers on page 34.

## Proper Mowing and Mower Care

Now, let's talk about mowing in July and August. Cut the lawn only once a week because the grass is not growing vigorously now. It is not necessary to pick up the clippings every week; leave the catcher off once in a while. Keep your mower set at the same height you began with in the spring. However, if your lawn is in poor shape and doesn't look too good, raise the blade slightly, as much as half an inch. For the stoloniferous grasses, such as bents and Bermudas, the blade should be left alone (not over three-fourths of an inch). Bare spots will be filled in by the grass's creeping "strawberry" habit of growth if you give them some attention. Never be tempted to lower your mower, no matter how cool the weather sometimes gets during July and August, and don't listen to contrary advice. Occasionally, like right after playing golf or watching TV golf played on a beautiful carpetlike turf, an enthusiastic homeowner suddenly lowers his mower to a scalping height. The home owner with the bent or Bermuda lawn can indeed get a close-cut turf if he begins the season with our recommended height of three-fourths of an inch or lower; but with bluegrass and other rhizome grasses, never. The bluegrass lawns around my clubhouse and the bluegrass rough on the course are never cut lower than two inches. Lowering the mower suddenly, especially during this time, is committing lawn murder. Grass develops a balance between the leaves and root system, and a sudden upset of this balance causes severe shock to the plant. Keep in mind that the chief function of the leaves is to make food for the plant. If this process is abruptly slowed, the plant dies or, in its weakened condition, is crowded out by weeds and attacked by disease. So don't lower your mower; raise it, if anything.

To check the setting on your mower, move the mower to a flat base, such as concrete or pavement. Then measure with a ruler from the bottom of the base to the top, or "lip," of the bed knife. Most mowers have notches that represent the various settings, and the blade can easily be raised and lowered by a simple adjustment with a wrench. This will also level your mower. You certainly don't want a lopsided cut.

Now that you're not cutting so frequently, check the sharpness of the reel blades by placing a dandelion leaf (taken from your neighbor's lawn, of course) between the bed knife and reel blades. Watch your fingers! If your mower is dull, get it sharpened. Now, more than ever, this is important. Grass is weakened by dull blades that pull and don't cut sharply, and the appearance of your lawn is marred.

If you have a rotary, use a twelve-inch fine bastard file to sharpen the blade. Put out your cigarette first! Move to some bare area. Gas and oil might leak out when you tip the mower to check the blade.

Wash your reel mower with hose and water after each use to avoid corrosion of the metal by grass juices. And don't get any water on the engine head.

Cut your lawn in the late afternoon or evening. Mowing is not recommended during high heat and humidity, not only for the sake of the grass, but also for your own comfort.

Touch up your mower with paint if it needs it. And check it for loose or worn-out parts.

Don't make sudden stops and starts, and don't cut when the lawn is saturated with water. It's too hard on the grass.

There is more information about lawn equipment on page 72.

## Tips for and Care of Summer Lawns

Sharpen gardening tools like shovels and hoes only on the inside tip, not on the back, as is commonly done; the edge will hold better.

Take inventory of your essential tools and replace whatever is necessary. You may also find that one or two other tools are now needed for your lawn and garden work. Although enthusiasm tends to prevail over common sense in the spring, if you hold out you'll find that tools are sometimes cheaper in the summer.

Arrange well in advance for mowing and watering while you're on vacation. Trust a young man, not a boy.

Give your small trees and ornamental shrubbery a heavy watering once every three weeks or so; for flowers, about once a week. Slowly turn on the faucet for your garden hose until the water barely trickles out, then place the end at the base of the plant for about three hours, after which time you move the hose to another tree. It's a good idea to wash dust off the leaves of your smaller trees and shrubbery once in a while; this opens up their "pores" and gives them a clean look. Some water, however little, is always taken through the leaf stomata, and this is what gives the leaves a freshened-up look right away.

Check your landscaping at this time. Are you satisfied with your trees and shrubs? Landscapers are not so busy now. Get at least three estimates.

Don't leave rugs, mats, or plastic swimming pools on your lawn during the hot weather for more than a few hours; otherwise the grass underneath will suffocate, and it may die. In most cases it will turn a mottled yellow and thin out. Move the kids' tent, too, at least every week.

## Mulch

During the middle of summer, when it's hot and dusty and humid and nothing looks fresh, improve the appearance of your lawn by cultivating around the grass edges, tree wells, and shrubbery edges. Then spread mulch on the bare areas where you have manicured. The grass is not growing helter-skelter now, so your edging will be neat for a long time. The mulch I recommend above any other is cocoa hulls. It's inexpensive and readily available at any landscape store. It also has the pleasant fragrance of cocoa, which, to me, always brings back memories of childhood days. For more on mulching, see page 77.

# A Swing Around North America

The weather is hot now, and this is a good time to relax. I want to take you on a little trip first to some provinces and states in North America so we can view their grasses.

## Canada

Our first stop is in western Canada, at Lethbridge, Alberta, just over the border from Montana. The main road joining the countries runs along one of the biggest Indian reservations (on both sides of the border) that I've ever seen. The Indians here raise some of the world's finest cattle. This area is also known for its Mennonites, a hard-working, cash-on-the-line people who have been a boon wherever they have settled.

Lethbridge's very rich and fertile soil is comparable to the land in the Bloomington area of Illinois. But Lethbridge is also known for the chinook winds—the warm winds that come over the Rocky Mountains and cause temperatures to soar from far below zero to well above melting in a very short time. I've walked to a hockey game wearing scarf and overcoat and, at the end of the game, walked home in my sports jacket. The chinook had come. During winter, of course, this wind causes intensive drying of plants, a major turf problem here. Dry soil, combined with dry air, increases the loss of moisture from dormant grass, which can shrivel and dry, particularly on slopes, banks, and other exposed surfaces. One thing the homeowners here can do to control this drying tendency is to cover the ground with brush to collect snow. Snow fences cut in half and set on the home lawn would also help. The best method, though, is to get out the hose after a prolonged dry period and water the lawn. However, it is also very important to water heavily just before the onset of winter. Dessication is much more of a problem on golf-course greens than on home lawns. The new practice of using polyethylene film to cover the greens in Canada is not satisfactory in the chinook area.

Merion is the most popular lawn grass here. In Canada, particularly in the west, Merion bluegrass takes longer to germinate and become established because of lower temperatures and a shorter growing season.

Let's go now to Saskatoon, Saskatchewan, which gets its name from the saskatoon berry, called Juneberry in the United States. A few years ago I acquired some rare saskatoon-berry seeds from Saskatchewan University and donated them to the Morton Arboretum in Illinois. In return, I was given some Illinois species that are now planted around the lakes at Briarwood Country Club in Deerfield, Illinois.

The area around Saskatoon is a prairieland like Illinois, except that Illinois is known for its hybrid corn and Saskatchewan for the best hard wheat in Canada. The prairie bunchgrasses used here for grazing are varieties of wheatgrasses, mostly crested. There are fescue and western porcupine grass, or "spear grass," as we used to call it. Although Merion bluegrass and Park bluegrass are grown in this area, I still recommend the common Kentucky bluegrass.

Will you wait for just a moment? This is the place of my youth. I caught my first gopher and snared my first rabbit here. I caught the elusive silvery goldeye and during the Depression helped my father carry home the prohibited "King's fish," the sturgeon. This is where the wild crocuses grow so profusely that they cover the prairies for miles in the spring. Here I saw the prairie chickens migrating from one area to another in the twilight of autumn, in flocks so thick that they blurred the sky. This is where I once saw the whooping cranes fly, and spent the nights of my youth reading the animal lore of Ernest Thompson Seton. But "you can't go home again," and we must leave.

Now we're in Winnipeg, Manitoba, our last stop in Canada, where we especially notice the beautiful elm trees. The dreaded Dutch elm bark beetle hasn't arrived yet, although its invasion is expected soon—it has already started elm disease in eastern Canada.

The native prairie grasses in Manitoba are bluestem, porcupine grass, panic grass, June grass, wheatgrass, and blue grama grass. They're called "prairie wool" by the farmers, and most are quite drought resistant. Homeowners here should not fertilize after September 15, thus allowing the grass to harden off for the harsh winter ahead. However, the lawn should be heavily watered before freezing temperatures set in.

Winnipeg has some of the most beautiful girls in Canada and also produces more hockey players than any other Canadian city, or so it thinks. If you ever visit this expanding, energetic city, be sure to ask if the gourmet's delight, the famous smoked Winnipeg goldeye, is available for your meal.

Before leaving Canada for the eastern United States, I'd like to mention that Toronto has both climate and grass problems very much like Chicago's. Consequently, pointers given for Chicago will also prove helpful north of Lake Erie.

## United States

In Maryland and the area around Washington, D.C., the weather can change from winter to hot summer very rapidly, with very little spring. Water restrictions are imposed almost every summer, partly because of the continuing shortage of water in the Potomac River. Southern grasses like Meyer zoysia and Bermuda can be grown; so can cool-region grasses. A transition zone, the area harbors many turf diseases, one being fusarium blight on Merion. Its circular, whitish-to-pink spots, half an inch and larger, can grow together and eventually take over the lawn. The White House lawn was lost to the disease in the summer of 1963, and this caused considerable concern to President Kennedy. There was and still is no really effective cure for the blight.

We are now in St. Louis, Missouri, heart of another twilight zone, where the weather gets very humid and where the grass is harder to grow than in any other place we will visit. Here the secret of a good lawn is never to cut the cool-region grasses under two and a half inches—even Merion—during summer. On the plus side in St. Louis, common bluegrass fares better under shade.

Next, a short visit in Kansas, the Wizard of Oz country, where tornadoes and violent winds are common. Both cool- and warm-region grasses grow well in areas of the state where the climate suits them: Bermuda in southern Kansas, and buffalo grass, a native, in western Kansas. Kentucky bluegrass does well in the northeast; below this region it overlaps with Bermuda. Common Kentucky bluegrass is the popular cool-region grass here. Varieties of the family, including Merion, have demonstrated no advantage over this sturdy, reliable strain.

Two important tips should be followed. With the cool-region grasses, be sure to mow, as in Missouri, no lower than two and a half inches. This practice will not only get your lawn through the stress periods better but it will also control the spread of crabgrass. Crabgrass moves rapidly into a cool-region rhizome grass that is cut short, but its growth is retarded in the shade of taller grass. This maintenance practice works here and in all states where crabgrass is a problem, although a height of two inches is permissible in northern states given over entirely to cool-region grasses. The second tip is applicable to all grasses, in all states and provinces, with special emphasis on states where both cool- and warm-region grasses can grow, as in Kansas. During prolonged drought, continue regular deep-root watering *even after a light shower.* Most homeowners let up, relieved that at last rain has come. But, my dear homeowner, unless the rain is heavy and penetrating (check your rain gauge), a light rain is as bad as shallow irrigation and does nothing but settle the dust. Letting up when the grass needs continued heavy watering allows the lawn to wilt and thin out; next comes invasion by crabgrass and other weeds; and then, saddest of all, the lawn sometimes is completely lost. So continue heavy, deep-root watering during hot and dry periods. Don't be put off by light showers or rains.

Now we're in "Wagon Train" country—Arizona and the great Southwest. We may wonder how lawns can grow in this land of sand and mesquite and cactus, but they do. In fact, excellent home lawns of both cool- and warm-region grasses are grown here. This land has high and low elevations, of course. At the high elevations Kentucky bluegrass varieties do well. At the lower, warm elevations, hybrid Bermuda is king. Cool-region grasses also are gaining favor for winter overseeding. At the high elevations of the state, common Kentucky bluegrass is noticeably different in color from any other Kentucky I have seen. It is a lighter blue-green, very refreshing to the eyes.

Interestingly, the time schedules for planting flowers and vegetables vary widely in Arizona because of differences in altitude. Depending on the elevation, planting dates can vary as much as three months. For example, at 2,500 feet or less above sea level, dahlias have planting dates from March to April and blossoming dates from April 15 to June. At 2,500 to 4,999 feet, planting dates are from July 1 to October 1, and you can count on the dahlias blossoming any time from July to frost. Remember, though, that organic matter, such as manure, decays fast in the sandy soil of the Southwest and should be replenished in your cultivated beds every year, rather than every two or three years as in the northern states.

Continuing westward, the first thing we notice about California lawns is that not all of them are grass. There are "lawns" of flowers, usually geraniums and carnations, and sometimes pebble stones painted green. There are entire lawns in southern California (also in Arizona) covered with a popular ground cover called *Dichondra,* a broad-leaved perennial that is related to the morning glories. *Dichondra* is planted in the spring; the heavier you seed, the better, if you want a fast crop. Luckily, with a height of two inches, it requires very little mowing or clipping. Cutworms can cause severe damage in new *Dichondra* lawns unless recommended insecticides are applied immediately at the onset of the attack. So watch for signs. Here, as in Arizona, both cool- and warm-region grasses can be grown. Californians like their lawns cut very short, and to meet this demand some dwarf bluegrasses are being developed.

Occasionally throughout the state a lawn will catch our eyes. The attraction in each case is a unique arrangement of grass and flowers and rock, the "Japanese garden" look—that distinctive blending of varieties of plants within a planned setting.

But it's time now to go home. Our little vacation is over and we need to take care of some important chores.

# September

WE ARE now approaching the homestretch of the growing season. The stress period for our grass is over. Oh, we'll still get hot days, many of them, but the humidity will be slowly replaced by invigorating dry air. There is less daylight now, and the September nights are longer and cooler—just what our turf loves. As we proudly look at our property, we notice that the grass is becoming revitalized, getting its second wind. The best of the seasons is starting, so don't let your enthusiasm wane. We have many interesting things to do.

## Fertilizing

The month of September is ideal for the final application of fertilizer on your lawn. Feeding cool-region grasses later than September often takes your turf into winter in a lush condition, with perhaps serious consequences. You don't want this to happen, because grass going into winter in a soft, lush condition is more susceptible to damage from snow mold, winterkill, and general traffic than is grass that has been fertilized earlier and has had time to harden off before the onset of winter. So don't fertilize your permanent grasses after

October 1 unless you are located in the extreme warm-region grass belt. In my opinion, the late-summer ("fall") application of fertilizer is the best and most important one of the year, because the roots get more of the benefits than does the top foliage, as is the case in the spring. In late summer and during the fall, as daytime temperatures wane and the nights become cooler and longer, the top growth of turf is reduced. Fnally, as late fall approaches, there is so little growth that the grass seems to be at a standstill, even though the temperatures are still mild enough to play golf. But all this time the roots keep right on growing, getting thick and full and groping deep into the earth. They are storing food for next spring, when they will again produce a vigorous, tight top growth—just what we're after. When the grass has been well nourished before winter sets in, the leaf system grows rapidly in spring and the root system expands as soil temperatures permit. There are other things in our favor now. New weeds have stopped growing and there is no worry about disease. So fertilize now with the plant food that is recommended on pages 36–39, and water it in.

## Aerifying

This is also a good time to aerify your lawn if its surface is compacted. An aerifying machine pulls out soil cores, and the holes permit better penetration of water, air, and fertilizer, resulting in deeper root development. It's a very good idea to sow grass lightly over any bare spots you may have right after aerifying, letting the grass seed fall into the holes. Grass will come up strong, fast, and with a tremendous root system.

## More Facts on Mowers and Lawn Equipment

Now is a very good time, too, to take a fresh equipment survey. Do you have anything that is falling apart or beyond repair? Ask yourself: Will the mower last for another season? Now, better than at any other time, you'll know; you have been using it all summer. And how about your old spreader and sprayer? What shape are they in? Price the many models of rotaries, reel mowers, riding mowers, garden tractors, and other equipment that's stored away unsold in the back rooms of hardware and garden stores. Believe me, your inquiries will be welcomed, and I guarantee you'll get a good price break. But, whatever you do, when buying a new piece of equipment be sure of service at the store and availability of parts by equipment companies.

**Hand mowers** are for small lawns, and they are very safe, inexpensive, and good exercise. And they're quiet.

**Rotary mowers** are able to cut high weeds and grass. Not only are they excellent for rough and semifine work, they can also do close trimming and mulch leaves in the fall. But though the rotary does a respectable job of mowing, it doesn't quite come up to the performance of a reel mower.

**Reel mowers** cut like scissors. Consequently, if the mower is sharp and adjusted properly, the grass blade is sheared cleanly and there is no ragged tip or wound. The tip heals quickly. This is why a lawn mowed with a reel mower looks better. It is a precision machine. For the homeowner who cares about formal appearance, the reel type is ideal. Another advantage is the roller in back, which rolls down worm castings and soil heaved up by freezing and thawing.

**Electric mowers** are limited, of course, by the length of the cord, as are electric cultivators, trimmers, and edgers. Be careful not to snarl or cut the cord or to mow when your grass is wet. Periodically check your cord for cuts and exposed wire. The electric machine is hard to maneuver if you have many trees; but it's easy to start, has no fumes, and is blessedly quiet.

**Riding mowers** are for larger than average lawns and estates. It's fun to ride one. However, never carry a child on your lap while mowing. Practice on level ground first, and always beware of tipping over while cutting steep slopes.

This is an appropriate place for some comments on fertilizer spreaders and chemical sprayers, and some good news for the homeowner on rental equipment.

The biggest improvement in **fertilizer spreaders** is the cyclone spreader, which uses the same principle as the cyclone hand seeder, except that you push this one and the fertilizer is fanned evenly to the front and sides in an eight-foot swath. The cyclone spreader is extremely accurate, easy to handle and clean, and is at least five times faster than ordinary spreaders. It makes all other applicators obsolete, so don't hesitate to buy one. The standard spinner type used for the average home lawn is priced very reasonably. It makes fertilizing a pleasure and practically eliminates all mistakes that can be made with the unwieldy buggy type and over-the-shoulder spreaders. It can also be used to spread seed, ice melters, herbicides, and granular or pelleted insecticides. Exercise care, though, not to spin herbicides near valuable plants.

There is also a big improvement in small **chemical sprayers.** The three-gallon hand pumper that you put over your shoulder has been outmoded by the three-gallon push type that sprays a neat pattern with wheel drive.

Although it's good to have the proper equipment always handy, what if you can't afford it or your storage space is limited? Perhaps you are contemplating a large renovation job, or performing a once-a-year job like aerifying, rolling, and edging the lawn, or rototilling a garden. What then? Well, the increasing availability of **rental equipment** is a real boon. I suggest that you rent the equipment and tools at one of the rental agencies. Many hardware and landscape-supply stores also rent garden equipment to homeowners for very reasonable rates. Check these before parting with your cash for something you can't afford or will seldom use.

## Putting in a New Lawn

Any day after August 15 is a good time to start your new lawn. You should even begin August 1 if you live in the northern states or Canada. However, I prefer the time right after Labor Day for the Chicago and the Midwest area. After the hot summer the soil is receptive to the grass seed. At this time damping-off, the sometimes disastrous disease of spring, is not a serious threat, except in southern lawns when winter grasses are overseeded. With less evaporation of moisture, there is less need for watering. Weed growth declines sharply. The chance of heavy rains and subsequent erosion has diminished. All the breaks come your way during this twilight of the summer season and the beginning of autumn, so start your new lawn now.

I will begin by describing how the lawn should be graded and seeded *properly,* whether you do it yourself, hire a landscaper, or have it done by the contractor of your new house. To avoid confusion, I'll start with the premise that you're building a new home. If you aren't, ignore some of these comments and apply only the advice that is needed.

To begin **preparation of the seedbed,** move the native topsoil to one side until the building is finished. When the subgrading is completed, get rid of all building debris, such as boards, paper, wire, workmen's beer cans, and bricks, on the site. Like children's toys, they can pop back and clutter up the lawn. Now move the topsoil back over the subgrade. The gradient should be gently sloped away from the house to provide adequate drainage. Grade the ground to the level of the sidewalk or driveway so the lawn mower doesn't hit the edges.

If you have any doubt about drainage, now is the time to tile, not after your lawn is in. Make this correction and grade out the mess that will occur from the digging. Get professional help on this if you're doing it yourself. The best source I've found is a local stone- and dirt-supply company. Most of these companies sell tile. And although I've installed miles of tile, I still go to my friends in the landscape-supply business when I'm not sure about a problem. So should you. Why not call your local golf-course superintendent? He will know who is best for drainage tiling.

Reliable dirt suppliers will help you estimate the quantity and correct mix of extra topsoil that might be needed for your new lawn. Remember, though, there is no such thing as cheap topsoil. Cheap soil is not high-quality soil. I caution you to be very careful of any "great buy" in topsoil. Quality topsoil has a 2-1-1 ratio: a mixture of two parts of good-quality dirt, one part sand, and one part humus. Incidentally, quality topsoil doesn't have to be black; in some states it's red. Ideal soil has a crumbly structure and is porous, with plenty of air space between soil particles. A good test is to squeeze slightly wet soil in your hand; quality soil will not form into a mud ball, but will fall apart. Another test is to drop a clump of soil from hip height; if it's good friable soil, it will fall apart. Have at least four inches of quality topsoil on your lawn. Measure the depth of several places with a ruler, especially if someone else is putting in the lawn.

The next step is to pulverize, level, and grade the topsoil with a power landscape rake. While the lawn is being graded, make sure the trunks of the trees are not covered high by soil. A few inches won't matter; but if too much soil is deposited around its base, the tree can die of root suffocation. Oak trees are particularly susceptible. The death of a tree is not immediate; it sometimes takes years, but the tree eventually dies. I've seen it happen too often. If a new lawn has to be higher than the base of the tree's trunk, build a circular well around the base with bricks or stone.

After the topsoil is graded, fine-rake it by hand in opposite, or cross, directions until the surface becomes perfectly level, with all stones picked up and all the lumps and bumps removed.

Now apply a 10-10-10 fertilizer at the rate of 20 pounds per 1,000 square feet (2 actual pounds of nitrogen, phosphorus, and potassium). Spread the nutrients in opposite directions and rake them in well. The whole secret of planting a good lawn is using enough fertilizer in combination with the grass seed. A lawn seeded without adding fertilizer will never amount to anything.

Now divide your seed in equal parts and sow it in opposite, or cross, directions, making sure no part of the seedbed is missed. Though I generally like to use chemicals at slightly less than the recommended dosage, I do the opposite with grass seeds and use half again as much to allow for seed lost or buried too deeply. In other words, if the recommendation is 4 pounds per 1,000 square feet, I will sow closer to 6 pounds of seed for the same area.

Don't be tempted by brightly colored seed packages with exaggerated phrases of promise and convenient handle grips. Just make sure the seed you buy is fine-textured and is certified premium seed. Believe me, no cheap seed will ever come close to giving you the beautiful home lawn that is pictured on its container. The law requires seed to be labeled fine-textured or coarse, so pick the best if you're after a superior lawn. Take nothing less. Low-priced or bargain seed often can be the most costly in the long run, because its purity and probability of germination are low. Except in special cases (see page 17), I recommend a pure, individual strain of grass seed rather than a mixture. Seed mixtures are cheaper because they are combined with useless grasses, one of which will dominate. I want you to strive for a first-class lawn and not be satisfied with less.

After the seed is sown, rake very lightly so it just settles in the depressions. If you're heavy-handed, or if you were at a party the night before, don't rake at all. (If you drink, don't rake!) The important note here is that the seed should not be pushed together or buried. More goes wrong at this point than at any other time. The homeowner will either miss sowing or fertilizing part of the lawn—that's why we do it in opposite directions—or bury the seed too deeply with too much raking.

Now, roll your lawn in several directions until it's firm. The heavier the roller, the better. Maybe you can get a neighbor to help. Make sure the soil is loose and dry so the dirt won't stick to the roller. Some seed will, but don't worry. And don't worry about the way the roller is compacting the soil; in fact, that's exactly what we want to do at this time. Seed will always germinate unless, of course, you have buried it too deeply. How many times have you seen grass or weeds come through the invisible cracks in cement or asphalt and marveled at its vitality? There are almost three million seeds in each pound of Kentucky bluegrass, so if you're sowing this, your chances that some will germinate are pretty good.

Now to the problems of **mulching** and erosion on gentle slopes. Mulching hastens germination by keeping the soil moist and warm. With a good mulch, the soil has less chance of drying or cracking, and a homeowner doesn't have to water so often. If you can get *weedfree* straw or hay (otherwise, forget it), spread one bale evenly over 1,000 square feet of lawn. Don't rake off the mulch. It will decompose while your seedlings grow, adding a little humus to your lawn. When the straw or hay becomes hardly noticeable, it's time to cut your lawn for the first time. The only drawback is that your neighbors might get sore if the mulch flies into their yard on a windy day. Keep it anchored with a crisscrossing of binder twine.

For sloped or terraced areas you will need potato sacks, ripped-open burlap bags, cheesecloth, or special mulching cloth or netting.

If you use potato sacks, take them off as soon as the seedlings come up; otherwise the tight weave will shut out sunlight and the weight will smother the young seedlings. Actually, I prefer to use clear polyethylene or plastic paper. The temperature under it becomes higher than on the outside, thereby rapidly incubating the seed and forcing a fast germination. Polyethylene can be purchased or ordered at your lumber store. Ask for four-millimeter thickness. However, the thinner protective covering placed around your clothes by the dry cleaner is perfect. Save it for the small slopes and bare areas where grass is having a hard time germinating. But before spreading the polyethylene cover, water these areas. Then, to keep the covers from being blown away by wind, make large staples from coat hangers. Stick them into the ground every twelve to eighteen inches at the edge of the plastic so the horizontal wire touches the plastic and is flush with the ground. As soon as the seedlings come up, as soon as you see green, take everything off—making sure that all the coat hangers are picked up, or your mower might be damaged by the imbedded wire the first time you cut the long young grass. If the plastic cover is left on the sprouting grass seedlings, heat and lack of air will smother them.

Although I've used this method for large areas, the homeowner should use the plastic "mulch" for only very small areas. The covering has to be picked up each time watering is needed, and over a large area it would be awkward. Even so, for slopes and banks there is nothing like plastic sheets for a fast overall coverage.

On **watering** a new lawn, I won't advise how much or when. Just keep the soil moist all the time, until the grass is an inch high—not saturated, puddled, or flooded—just moist. And use planks to walk on while watering. When the grass is about one inch high, taper off your watering. Too much water will cause seedbed erosion. Reach a happy medium with the watering so your seedbed is neither washed out nor dry and cracked. With underwatering, the young seedlings will usually shrivel and die.

The **first mowing** should be done when the new grass reaches two inches, and definitely before it reaches three inches. The first mowing should be in the fall before frost comes; the second mowing will be in the spring. I recommend that you use a reel mower for the first two times. After that go back to your rotary. However, if the fall season is exceptionally long and warm, and your grass again reaches three inches, then mow one last time. The grass shouldn't go into the winter longer than two inches. Avoid tearing the young grass by using a very sharp reel mower, and make sure the lawn is almost dry when you mow. Late afternoon is best. Remove the clippings.

During **the lawn's first year** the only FERTILIZER that should be applied to it is organic fertilizer. This is to prevent any possibility of burning the young lawn. But more important, this will provide a slow, steady growth and maintain a balance between root-zone and top-foliage growth. Fertilizer should be applied three times after the first winter, each time using 2 pounds of actual nitrogen per 1,000 square feet. The times for the three applications are the first week in May, the first day of summer, and right after Labor Day.

Now is a good time to remind you that during the first winter you should permit no traffic to compact the young grass. Keep children, wheelbarrows, and machines off the lawn, and keep sleds and toboggans off the slopes. The immature roots of grass are easily harmed by traffic during the winter months. Not only that; snow mold likes to start in footprints and other depressions.

The time has finally come to give you, as I promised on page 54, the one important reason—aside from initial cost—why THE SODDED LAWN may be less preferable than a seeded lawn. Turf produced from seed develops a deeper and denser growth of roots and better foliage than does turf established from sod, due to a better relationship between the roots and the leaves from the time the shoots of grass first break ground to the time the grass becomes mature. In sodding, the mature turf is punished severely by the stripping of its established root system and by the loss of that ideal balance between root and leaf established prior to the cutting. The turf never quite reaches that ideal relationship again. For now, in the sodded lawn of dissimilar soil, development of foliage precedes development of root, and the weakened root system is hard pressed to support the foliage. Careful watering and fertilizing practices will develop a stronger root system, but otherwise, ill effects can result from this imperfect relationship. A reasonably close balance must be achieved. The tendency to add a lot of nitrogen to the sodded lawn does nothing but stimulate and increase the top growth, while the root zone remains weak and shallow. However, if nitrogen levels are kept low, the root production is increased, the top growth is showed, and our efforts toward a reasonable balance begin to be successful.

Therefore, during the first year a low-nitrogen-content fertilizer or a very slow-releasing one should be used on the sodded lawn. Better yet, use none at all and give the roots time to become more fully developed, and thus make use of the fertilizer that went into the preparation of the sod bed.

WEEDS in the new lawn can be eradicated in spring if the homeowner applies herbicides carefully and knows what he is doing. However, I suggest that the average homeowner wait a full year—over to the next spring—before applying weed killers. Meanwhile, pull out the weeds by hand. Weeds in a young soft lawn come out easily and it's great exercise for your wife and children, while you supervise.

## Making a Soil Test

You might ask at this time why such soil additives as lime, sawdust, mica, calcined clay, and others were not recommended for seedbed preparation. The answer is that you rarely need any of them if top-quality soil was used. The paramount reason for using top-grade soil was to eliminate the necessity for purchasing expensive supplements. A complete fertilizer is all your topsoil needs. Why add all that other junk? And that's just what it is if you don't need it—junk. Remember, my friend, beautiful lawns were built many years before the advent of the supplements now heralded as panaceas for poor topsoils. The old lawns were good lawns because only good soil was used.

As for the soil's being alkaline or acid, only a reliable soil test can tell. Unless the soil in your area has a reputation for being strongly acid or alkaline (New England soils, for example, are quite acid and almost automatically need lime), I recommend that you take the soil test after the ground has settled uniformly, after it has been washed with rain, watered artificially during the summer, mowed a few times, and has a thick carpet of green. At that time, by reading the soil analysis, you will be able to determine what you need and supply it easily to the turf—that is, of course, *if you need anything.* Liming a lawn without a soil test, no matter how little, is foolish and a waste of time and money. Lime and some trace elements should be applied only on the basis of professional soil tests. But every homeowner should do one or have one done, even if only for the satisfaction of being absolutely sure that he doesn't need this, that, or something else.

I realize that most lawn experts advise the homeowner to make a soil test during seedbed preparation. But not made explicit is when or at what step (and exactness is very important) you are supposed to obtain samples for the test. Should they be taken when the soil is stockpiled at the "dirt yard" or when it's dumped in your yard? Or at the time of rough grading, or when the lawn is fine-raked and leveled? Of course, if the tests show that lime or something else is required, then you'll have extra raking to do to mix the lime into the soil. But you should realize that while the beautiful seeding days fly by, you'll be sitting and waiting for the results of your soil tests to come in. And just when they arrive, so, perhaps, will the rain. Boy, what a mess! It happens all the time. Look, the building of a new lawn is an operation that has to be done at one time. There must be no delay from start to finish. The weather might change, and each day lost brings you closer to winter. Forget the soil test now, unless you are in an extremely acid or alkaline locality. Get it done when you have plenty of time.

Here's the way to take a soil sample. First, rent or borrow a sampling soil probe from a lawn- or golf-supply company. Then at ground level, not thatch level, take twelve plugs (if you have an average lawn) exactly two inches deep from various parts of your lawn. Uniformity of the samples is very important; otherwise your reading will be misleading. Because different minerals, mainly phosphorous and potassium, occur at different levels, a two-inch depth is specified to get reliable results. The samples now should be dried, mixed thoroughly, tagged, and sent to a good soil-testing laboratory. Of course, if you have an extremely large area of different soils, you may want to take soil tests of different sections. In that case, intact plugs can be put separately into small paper bags and marked individually for proper identification upon their return.

The best way to find out where to send your soil samples is by consulting your local county agricultural agent or writing to the state university extension department. You may also consult the local garden-store operator, the neighborhood garden club, or your favorite golf-course superintendent. The charge is either small or nothing at all. The best time to take the soil tests is in the fall, when most of your maintenance work is over and you have time for sampling. After you receive the results, the winter months can be used to plan a spring program if additives are indicated. Take a soil test every three years.

I don't recommend that soil tests be run with home kits. Home kits are often inaccurate. For something as important as your lawn, testing should be done by a responsible lab with trained personnel. In home kits the glassware becomes dirty, chemicals lose strength, and color charts fade. Few homeowners get refills regularly. Worst of all, there is human error. However, if you are an enthusiast, have a soil analysis done by a scientific laboratory and do one yourself with a home kit. Compare the results and see how close you came.

## How to Build a Home Putting Green

The growing enthusiasm for golf has brought to the homeowner a new luxury item, the home putting green. Many golfers are installing one so they can sharpen their putting whenever they have a spare moment. And why not? It's half the game, and it can be practiced at home. In fact, everyone in the family can enjoy a private green. Developers of high-rise apartments and motel owners are finding that putting greens are paying off in happy customers. In Fort Lauderdale, for example, most of the popular apartments have a small putting green next to the swimming pool. And you haven't lived until you've practiced putting on a green in the wild blue yonder, as I did last year, ten stories above Chicago.

Over the years I have built many home putting greens and a few four- and five-hole golf courses on large estates. Because they are definitely a luxury and require special knowledge, it's best to have professional people build one for you. However, you may wish to try it yourself, and if you do, this is the way.

First, forget about starting a putting green from seed, unless you're experienced in the growing of putting-green turf, such as the bents and Bermudas. You won't make it if you're not. You'll have a much better chance of success with sod. Use bent, unless you live in the South, in which case use Bermuda.

Pick a sunny location with good drainage. The **size** should be anywhere from 500 square feet to 1,000 square feet for the average lot. This is the most popular size. Anything over that will usually be out of proportion with the rest of the yard and start to cost important money and time for maintenance. Stake out the area for the putting green, preferably in a circle. Then have the existing lawn turf taken off with a sod cutter. Use the grass you took off to sod bare spots in your lawn or anywhere else that needs sodding. Look around your yard—you'll find a few such places.

Now order 3 cubic yards of top-quality **topsoil** for a minimum-sized green (500 square feet) and 5 cubic yards for the maximum size(1,000 square feet). Tell your dirt dealer what you want it for, and get the very best. Ask him to deliver the topsoil in a small truck if possible. Have it dumped in the center of your "target" when the lawn is hard and dry so the truck can go over the grass without doing damage (placing boards underneath the truck wheels will help), or else dump the dirt on the asphalt as near as possible to the green site and wheel it in with a barrow.

If you're still able to go on after this strenuous effort, you can begin **shaping the surface.** But first go into the kitchen and get one of your wife's dinner plates. Not the deep kind—just an ordinary shallow plate, without any ridges. Now turn the plate upside down and study it, noting the contour. Shape your green just like the plate. Forget the waves, rolls, and undulations of larger golf-course greens you've seen and putted on. Your green is too small for that; keep it flatter and simple. Be sure the edges of the green are gently sloped to prevent scalping. However—and this is very important—shape the surface so it drains quickly away with the slope or incline of the land. I can't emphasize this point too strongly. What about tile? Unless your property is completely flat, you won't need tile for one of these small greens if you work with the slope of the property.

Now rake a double dose of 10-10-10 **fertilizer** into the upper two inches of soil and use a roller on your sod bed over and over again. Between rollings, rake the surface until all depressions are out and the top is perfectly smooth. Remember, your putting-green turf will be very short, and the slightest undulation will show after the turf is laid. Make the soil so compact by the continuous rolling that when you walk on it your feet won't sink in.

Next, measure your area very carefully again and order the **sod**—bent or Bermuda—from a reputable nursery. The sod might take awhile to be delivered, but that's all right; the more time your architectural masterpiece has to settle, the better. When the sod comes, lay it, roll it a few times, and spread organic fertilizer—1 pound actual nitrogen per 1,000 square feet—over its top. Keep the sod watered. Bent likes plenty of water, but it must have excellent drainage.

I recommend the purchase of an English **greens mower,** made especially for putting greens. One of the landscape or sod dealers will know where to get one of these precision push machines. (They can also inform you where to get cups and flags for your green.) I don't know of any American firm that makes a push mower which can be set low enough to cut greens. I definitely advise you not to use a power greens mower (easily available but expensive) unless extensive lessons are given is its handling. They are extremely hard to maneuver on small areas, and the homeowner might do more damage than good to his grass and himself.

During **the first days,** roll the sod a couple of times every three days just before watering. On the tenth day, mow it. I wouldn't advise cutting under one-fourth of an inch or over three-eighths of an inch. Proper adjustment and sharp blades are essential. Once the sod is established, cut it a minimum of twice a week—although every second day would be ideal—and always use a catcher to pick up the clippings. Have a soil test taken the first year.

Sounds easy? Well, I have one more suggestion. And unless this is done, I recommend that you forget about building your own home putting green. Call a golf-course superintendent, or some other qualified expert, and ask him to work out a **maintenance program** with you for disease, topdressing, fertilizer, and insects. Your green won't survive without this. Believe me, I am not trying to discourage you. My whole aim in this book is to give you the facts, not to paint a picture of false simplicity. I always give my home-putting-green customers a one-year guarantee, during which time I also show them how to maintain their greens. After the first year, the homeowner usually does quite well by himself.

There are many landscape companies and people who will build home putting greens. But after installation they charge for service calls when the green has problems. A word of caution: unless the homeowner receives advice on what to do after the green is built, and some return calls by the builder to see how it's doing the first year, he will discover that the easiest part of the whole operation has been only the actual building of the home putting green. The reliable builder guarantees service.

# October and November

AS WE step outside to finish our last garden chores, we hear the distant lonely cry of the mourning dove, as if coming from some lost woodland, and there is a sudden spellbound stillness. A shiver comes over us. We feel a great lonesomeness, a sadness. This strange feeling of something lost stays only a fleeting moment, then is gone. What is it? What is it? we ask. Then we feel the chill wind and hear the faint rustle of the tossing leaves, and we know—summer is gone.

> Like flames upon an altar shine the sheaves;
> And, following thee, in thy ovation splendid,
> Thine almoner, the wind, scatters the golden leaves!
> —HENRY WADSWORTH LONGFELLOW, "Autumn"

As the farmer comes to the end of his harvest, we now come to the twilight of the mowing season. The farmer reaps from his land the dividend of his labor. But what do we reap? What is our accomplishment? What is our reward, that after working all summer long to make our yard look beautiful, it comes to this: an area browned, piled with leaves, and rimmed with withered flowers? Yes, it would seem fruitless, except for one thing. We really didn't anticipate a reward of material things. We enjoyed what we did and got pleasure from our efforts in our "field of green," and we hoped, too, that our efforts pleased the eyes of other men. Yes, all this, and such fair memories of summer's warm loveliness that they will linger through the long winter and inspire us, in spite of ourselves, to start again the planning and dreaming and weaving of our next garden, held fast in the enchantment of each and every spring. This is our reward.

There is something else. Nature has a way of soothing and calming the troubled mind. The grass, birds, flowers, and trees—each has a way of making the mind peaceful and at ease. This is nature's therapy, and it is equal to any other. Let us not get so involved in hectic work, sometimes selfishly, that we forget to kneel down once in awhile to run the soil through our fingers or listen to the breeze from meadow and woods, the soothing sound of the Shepherd's flute. While the farmer reaps the harvest of his crop, we reap a harvest of our own—peace of mind.

Most homeowners associate the fall season with raking leaves. Sure, it's time-consuming, especially during the weekends when there is an endless parade of football games to watch. Don't worry. Raking is necessary only once, when all the leaves are off the trees. Then rake and burn them. An excellent way of celebrating the end of this job is to make a big pile of leaves for the children to jump into, and then use the pile for roasting marshmallows.

Because leaves that fall in the shrubbery and garden and in tree wells make a good mulch, leave them there. This is natural mulch, and the best. Now, when all the leaves have fallen, it's time for your final mowing of the grass after raking.

## Some Final Chores

We are now at the end of our chores, except for a few very important ones.

If your grass is dry, give it a very heavy watering before the ground freezes. Even though many authorities advise the homeowner to water only evergreens, I recommend that you water *all* small deciduous trees and ornamental shrubbery before freeze-up. And when you finish this, spray your grass against snow mold.

Finally, put away your mower in *perfect* operating condition. The lawn mower is the "final touch" in turf maintenance, so it deserves proper care. Instead of waiting until the middle of winter or spring, take your mower to a dependable shop for a checkup and sharpening at the close of the mowing season. Ask for an itemized bill for any repair work.

As soon as the mower is back, fill it with fresh gasoline and oil just before you put it away. I know this contradicts the time-honored practice of draining the fuel from gasoline-powered equipment before storing it, and running the engine dry to prevent gums and varnish from forming in the fuel tank and carburetor. The effectiveness of this old method varies, though, because the owner really does not run all the fuel from the engine. Some remains in the carburetor and fuel bowl and in the pickup inlet at the bottom of the fuel tank. Then the remaining fuel dries, leaving gummy deposits in these three critical places. In addition, the seals and gaskets in the carburetor and fuel-line hoses tend to dry out and cause gasoline leaks in spring.

Therefore, follow the lesser of two evils: fill the power unit with fresh gasoline, and after draining the crankcase refill it with the proper amount of new oil. It also would be helpful to remove the spark plug and put in about a teaspoonful of crankcase oil, then pull the starter through three or four times to coat the cylinder walls and prevent rust.

The storage area affects the condition of a power unit during winter. Machines stored near high heat—behind the furnace, for instance—will have more than normal evaporation; units stored in damp places will have a lot of internal rusting.

Close the fuel-tank shutoff so tightly that if the fuel bypasses the carburetor, only the fuel in the carburetor will leak. This may not seem important, but it greatly reduces the chance of fire.

Now we come to the end of the trail. It has been a good year for our program of growing a "golf-course" lawn. We have disregarded all the commercials and advertising along with the expert advice from friendly neighbors. We left the well-trodden path here and there, perhaps because we heard "a different drummer" and, by stepping to his tune, emerged at a prettier place.

We tackled our problems resolutely and with determination. It wasn't always easy. We had our contests with Mother Nature and she won a few bouts, as she always does, and forever will. Maybe that was the best lesson of all. We followed the book closely, and everything fell into place. The expense was smaller than in past years, and the anxiety was less.

If you have been having success with your lawn, and with the rest of the plantings, then don't change your formula. Continue what you have been doing. You must be on the right track, and I wish you continued success.

The days are shorter, and the leaves float down like magic carpets. The days are mild and hazy, with nature's kaleidoscope of color seen along streets and lanes. There is the fragrance of autumn in the burning leaves. These are the melancholy, lovely days of the most beautiful season—Indian summer. It will last a short time only. Enjoy it! This is Mother Nature's farewell to us, and she makes it so lovely that we can wait content for the promise of spring. Always at this time I wait for the *Chicago Tribune* and its annual printing of John McCutcheon's classic cartoon, "Injun Summer." Every year I read its legend to my children. The newspaper boy has just dropped it at my doorstep. Excuse me, I am about to read it now.

# City Lawns

IN THIS chapter I have some specific suggestions for the owners of homes deep in the heart of the city. Most lawn and garden books pitch their appeal to the suburbanite, and no wonder, for when a man moves to the suburbs he immediately becomes conscious that the emphasis is on classic lawns and landscaping. When the first thing he hears on being introduced to his neighbor is "What are you going to do about your lawn?" he instantly realizes that two cars, mink for his wife and daughter, and a son in Harvard are not enough to guarantee prestige here.

City homes are usually built close together and have small lawns. Space is at a premium. But city dwellers know how to work in their close quarters, and I've seen beautiful lawns in front and productive vegetable gardens in the backyard. Many are showplaces, with attractive flower boxes and flower borders. However, the slightly higher temperatures and the concentration of carbon monoxide and smog, along with dust and litter, make any city tough on plants as well as on human beings.

Certain trees can exist in the special conditions of the city better than other types. They also can endure having concrete close to their bases. These trees are the silver and red maple, the locust, and the linden. Another tree that thrives in spite of soot and smoke and smog is the ailanthus, familiar to readers of Betty Smith's *A Tree Grows in Brooklyn.* The ailanthus is Chinese in origin and is a somewhat weedy tree if not controlled. It lets nothing faze it and finds moisture and sustenance where nothing else can grow. Among evergreens, the Japanese yews tolerate the city better than most. But in the city, every two weeks or so in favorable weather, all trees and shrubs should have the soot washed off their leaves with a hose. The particles of soot block sunlight, plug the leaf pores, and smother the plant.

Flowers that do well in a city are sweet alyssum, ageratum, petunias, salvia, and geraniums. A city homeowner should be careful not to plant anything that isn't tolerant of the shade between homes or other buildings where there are little space, sunlight, or air movement. In places like this, I would recommend a Japanese rock garden. Another idea is the use of concrete flower boxes; they perk up spaces between buildings.

The city dweller who is building a new lawn finds soil more expensive and harder to get than in the suburbs because it usually has to be hauled from a distant site. The temptation is to use earth from nearby excavations, but such soil is rarely suited to lawn building.

Although there has been a tremendous amount of vandalism in cities—and in suburbs, too, of course—I have observed that well-kept lawns and flower beds attract less litter and less destruction than weed-filled plots. Most city dwellers appreciate efforts to make an attractive yard. Many cities, too, are carrying out beautification programs, especially in the slum areas, with planting programs for children, many of whom have never seen a growing vegetable or flower, a bee or a butterfly. May the city fathers continue their good work in this as well as other areas.

The home buyer moving to a new city should investigate his immediate area and see what plants are growing well. Plant species can change within five miles or less, particularly on the windward side of an industrial area. (Stay away from such a place if you have respiratory problems.)

Often mistaken for a grass disease, injury from dog urine is a frequent problem in the city. Dogs as a rule use any lawn except their own. Therefore, if you have a dog and your neighbor doesn't, you're one up. If you both own dogs, you're even. But if he has a dog and you haven't, buy a fence or a dog. If you own a dog, another solution is to have a dog station, usually consisting of a dirt box or a section of roped-off ground.

# Miscellaneous Tips

THROUGH THE years of growing and tending turf you learn a large amount of small ways that will help in getting something extra out of grass. Although a number of tips appear throughout the book, this is a good place to pass on more of them, plus special suggestions about renovating run-down lawns and dealing with lawn-service people.

## Renovating Run-Down Lawns

If your lawn has become run-down owing to poor maintenance practices, fertilize it every month, beginning in May and ending in September. Use a complete fertilizer at the start and finish (as recommended on page 37.) For the months in between, use an organic fertilizer, 1 actual pound of nitrogen per 1,000 square feet. The fertilizer will thicken the sparse, thin lawn and fill in the bare patches. However, if the patches are more than six inches in diameter, seed or sod them. Water your lawn properly, and don't do anything else —no aerifying, no verticutting, no adding of chemicals, no nothing, except adequate fertilizing and watering. If you follow these directions, and if your lawn isn't too far gone, you'll be pleasantly surprised by fall. However, if your lawn appears to be 50 percent gone, forget it. Plow it under and start again. Don't fool yourself into spending more time and money—the lawn's too far gone and will never be more than an embarrassing eyesore.

For more information on establishing and maintaining lawns, you have the extension service of the local state agricultural college or university. These land-grant colleges are maintained to serve you, and they do so through their many booklets and other informative data on lawn care. There are also many booklets you may request from the Office of Information, U.S. Department of Agriculture, Washington, D.C. 20250; these are inexpensive and some are free. Just ask for the USDA lawn-maintenance booklet, or the various booklets on tree and landscape care, and control of lawn insects and disease. There are numerous county cooperative extension service offices in each state. Illinois, for example, has over 100; Florida, 67; Minnesota, 96; Washington, 36. I've called a few, and believe me, they are most willing to help you with everything from crabgrass to canning preserves.

## Gardeners and Lawn Services

Most homeowners do their lawn work themselves, although many have gardeners or have their lawns maintained every week by lawn-service companies. Satisfactory gardeners are hard to find, and you are fortunate if you have one. Years ago it was a matter of pride and craftsmanship to spend the time and make the effort to manicure a property carefully and meticulously. Today, many gardeners and landscape companies come in and do the work quickly, even sloppily, and get out fast. Watch out for the fly-by-night operators; they generally have no professional background and can cause great damage to your property. If a lawn "expert" does poor work on the first day, get rid of him.

How can you make sure performance is good? First, hire a reputable company. It might charge more per hour, but usually it has superior help and first-class equipment. An efficient use of labor and equipment actually may result in a considerably lower cost. A top-grade landscape gardener takes pride in his work and reputation. He pays good wages to his help and won't tolerate sloppy work or lazy, inefficient performances. The qualified lawn-service company doesn't want to lose a good account or its hard-earned reputation. Word gets around fast when homeowners are pleased with efficient maintenance. Keep in mind that the hourly rates for labor and equipment are based on a seasonal business.

When first hiring a lawn service, talk with the owner and tell him what you want. Have him introduce you to the man who will be in charge of your lawn. Explain clearly to both of them what you want done, and make it clear that you won't be satisfied with anything less than top performance. If you have a justifiable complaint (not just because you woke up on the wrong side of the bed), don't wait and don't complain to the help. Call or see the head man and tell him about the problem—it's your money and his reputation.

This also is a good time to caution you about door-to-door humus and black-dirt hucksters and about gyp tree and sod salesmen, on all of whom thousands of dollars a year are wasted. To peddle their bargain dirt they usually bring a sample of peat soil to the door in a pail or basket and ask the homeowner to run his fingers through the lovely stuff. Outside stands a truck with what looks like good topsoil, but it's often inferior dirt thinly covered by good loam. The homeowner is convinced he is getting a good deal, pays the man, and has a load of worthless fill dirt full of weed seeds dumped on his property. Sometimes the homeowner pays on the promise the dirt will be delivered next day, and neither the dirt nor the money is seen again. Another trick is to dump a load of the very best soil, sold for a reasonable price, at a home, and then, after word gets around about the great "bargain," the gyp dealer comes back and, believe it or not, sells the whole neighborhood. (For this trick they prefer new housing developments.) After the big sale—cash in advance, of course—the dealer dumps worthless soil or promises to come back tomorrow and then never shows up. I could go on, but you get the idea. Don't be hoodwinked by the country clothing, the folksy talk, the barnyard odor, or the homey impression that the fellow is doing you a great favor with his surplus farm soil for just a few bucks. Forget it!

We come now to an often asked question: How can I lighten my lawn-service bill? The way to lighten it the most, of course, is for you and your family to do the work. However, even if you are able to afford quality service, the bills often get out of hand, and naturally you wonder how you can bring them down to a more reasonable level.

First, if you regard gardening as a hobby, or as a good sedative before going to bed, then you can do minor chores like cultivating flower beds and weeding. Have the lawn-service company do the basic jobs.

Another way to save money comes during July and August, when the grass is semidormant. During this period, tell your gardener or landscape company not to pick up grass clippings. Picking and hauling away clippings each time is time-consuming and costly. Besides, they add nutrients to the soil—again saving you money.

Lastly, remember my advice and recommendations on fertilizers, weeds, insects, and when specific tasks should be done and what to use. Of course, you have to be a little flexible and work with the methods most suitable for your area. However, keep my basic instructions in the back of your head and don't be pushed by fast-talking authoritative voices into paying for maintenance work you don't need.

The best time to look for a lawn-service company is during the summer. Don't be so sure you can hire a good one, though, that you discontinue your old service before you have a definite commitment from another one, unless you're willing and able to do all the work yourself for a time—in which case you wouldn't be looking for a lawn-service company, would you? Have something in the fire and keep your eyes and ears open during the summer as you walk or ride around. Watch how the men go about their work on the other estates and lawns. Are several of them standing around while one works? Do they all stop work and go for a drink of water together or stop for smokes like a group after a P.T.A. meeting? Or are they steadily keeping busy—not hurrying, but steady? If you like what you see, find out the name of the company, talk to some of its customers, and then call the owner. Even if he is booked up (and he usually is), he will make an effort to fit you into his schedule or place your name on his list for the future. If you get nothing out of it but the experience, that alone is usually worth the time and effort, and you might find out how well off you are with the service you already have.

There are a number of generally successful ways to find good gardeners. A personal recommendation by a friend or neighbor is perhaps the easiest and quickest. Or you can advertise for a retired man; but don't take the first one that comes—see several and give each a tryout before hiring one. Then there may be servicemen stationed near your town. There are always some who are glad for a chance to pick up extra money after hours, and, incidentally, their wives are good baby-sitters.

And now, Mom and Dad, I will let you in on an unrivaled source of gardeners. That fellow—the one with the long hair, the one you have fed and clothed all his life, the one to whom you have given too large of allowance. The one with the strong, tanned torso who's on his way to "where the girls are." The one who is quick to protest about the conditions of the world. Your son, Mother and Father. Your boy, who is bored, maybe spoiled, and usually complaining of nothing to do. Give him something to do. There is your gardener, and you have paid him many, many times. It's his turn now. Oh, J. D. Salinger, what has happened to the children playing in your fields of rye? What has happened to your "Catcher"? Where is he? Some of the children are falling over the precipice! But you, Mom and Dad, can catch one for your lawn work.

## A Potpourri of Tips

Hard-to-cut grass between fences is made easier to mow by digging a trench three inches wide and almost as deep next to the fence and filling it with crushed limestone or cocoa hulls.

Train your grass by cutting frequently at a uniform height but in different directions, so as to avoid making a pattern. Your grass should stand up, not be pushed one way all the time.

Don't walk over frosted grass, because the frozen cells of the grass blades will be crushed; the resulting black footprints will take a long time to recover.

Cutting your lawn while the early-morning dew is still on it will result in clumps of clippings, plus wet shoes. Grass stays healthier when cut in the afternoon or early evening, and your neighbor will be healthier—and friendlier—if he gets his sleep.

During the May and June growing season, manicure the borders of your lawn to give your place a meticulous look. A good way to eliminate grass in sidewalk cracks is to pour a little gasoline over it.

Trees absorb a lot of fertilizer from the grass under them, leaving famine areas that look thin and scraggly. Take care of this condition by fertilizing twice around the trees each time you fertilize your lawn.

For those of you who are allergic to grass—that's right, I am!—use a face mask or a doubled handkerchief when applying pesticides or fertilizer. Wear gloves, and change clothing right after handling chemicals. Take it easy when grass pollenates (from the last week in May to July) and get someone else to cut the lawn. In August and September, the ragweed season, take an ocean cruise.

Before taking a hot bath or shower, move your house plants into the bathroom with you for a steam bath. They love humidity. Catch rain water for your house plants and give them a treat once in awhile. The soft water will also do wonders for the wife's or daughter's hair.

To help cut flowers stay fresh as long as possible, cut the stems on a slant and change the water every day, using only lukewarm water. Add a little flower preservant. The old wive's tales of adding aspirin or household detergent to the water don't work. A little sugar does.

Grass stains? A little common rubbing alcohol will take care of grass stains on cotton and colorfast materials. Follow this with regular washing and no more stain.

# Gardens

WHILE WE are still on the subject of beautifying the lawn, let's agree to put aside a small plot of ground for a garden, in full sun. Although this book is primarily about lawns, I'll endeavor to give some advice on a few other things that go with lawns, like vegetable gardens, flowers, trees.

## Vegetable Gardens

In recent years, people have been getting away from gardens, devoting their property to solid lawns and ornamental landscaping. I believe the enthusiasm for vegetable gardens started to decline right after the end of World War II (remember the Victory gardens?), when vegetables again became abundant on the market. While scarcity and high cost are no longer strong motives, growing vegetables can still give real satisfaction.

I'll tell you how to grow only one vegetable, **the tomato.** The rest I'll leave to garden experts and their good advice. Start slowly at first with the easy vegetables, like carrots, radishes, and lettuce. Follow the directions on the packages, and you'll be surprised.

However, the tomato, a choice ingredient of every salad, is one popular vegetable that requires more care than others for best results. I'll tell you how my mother, the greatest gardener I know, grew the most abundant, the biggest, the most delicious tomatoes I've ever seen or tasted. My mother began her gardening in the black soils of the Ukraine, and she forgot nothing at all on the long trip over to this continent.

First, work some dried manure into the soil. (This fertilizer should be replenished every two years.) Now dig bowl-bottomed holes, spacing them two feet apart from outside edge to outside edge. The holes should be one and a half feet in diameter and five inches deep. Bank the soil around the outside of the hole to hold in the water. At the garden store select some starter plants about six to eight inches high with thick stems and good root systems that will withstand the wind. Now, carefully place a third of their stalk height into the holes; that's right, one-third of the stalk. Pat earth around the base. Cover the small plants when there's a chance of frost or strong winds. The best protection is a little shelter of three or four shingles placed around each plant, but little boxes will also serve the purpose. You can take them off when the sun is shining. To water the young roots, use a sprinkling can filled with lukewarm water. Direct the stream into the hole, never over the top of the tomato plant; otherwise you might, unfortunately start rot and yellowing of the plants.

When the tomatoes are deep-rooted and getting high, take off the shingles or boxes and cultivate the plants. Use a hose now to water them, slowly, whenever they are dry. (My mother used water from an old rain barrel.) This is the time to buy some five-foot laths—or you can use sturdy sticks of the same size—and stake your tomatoes. Drive the stakes firmly into the ground to a depth of one foot. Using strips of rag or lengths of soft twine, make your first snug tie at three-quarters the height of the plant. As the vine grows up the stick, tie your plant twice more. It's very important now to pinch out all new growths and shoots on the sides of the plant. Just be sure to leave all the growth on top; this will encourage fruiting of the main stem and make for an abundance of flowers and large tomatoes. Try it.

## Flower Gardens

Almost every homeowner who has a lawn also has flowers growing in his yard, along with a tree or two. This is as it should be, for grass, flowers, and trees are a perfect blend. In Sir Arthur Conan Doyle's short story "The Naval Treaty," Sherlock Holmes (who could have run circles around James Bond) picks up a rose and says:

> Our highest assurance of the goodness of Providence seems . . . to rest in flowers. All other things . . . are all really necessary. . . . But this rose is an extra. Its smell and its colour are an embellishment of life, not a condition of it. It is only goodness which gives extras. . . .

Flowers should never be planted until the chance of frost is past. In the Chicago climate, any time after May 20 usually is safe. How many flowers and what kind are up to you. I only suggest that you start by planting in large splashes for a mass effect and a professional touch, rather than packing many varieties together and having a "garbage bed."

The flowers most dependable and easiest to grow are **petunias.** Buy them in flats. You can't go wrong with petunias.

The flower easiest to grow from seed is the **moss rose,** usually called portulaca. Strew the portulaca seeds by hand over a carefully raked seedbed. Do not cover them; just keep them moist. When they start to sprout, water the seedlings whenever you think about it. They make a beautiful mass growth for very little money and very little care.

Curved flower beds make for easier lawn mowing than beds with right angles.

Why not **wild flowers** in your yard? This is fine, of course, but the best way to enjoy wild flowers is to observe them in their natural habitat. Photograph flowers; they don't run away. Leave them, for enjoyment of flowers is something to be shared with others, and as long as we realize this our wild flowers will be safe.

I should say that **the tulip** is one of my favorite flowers, and the late fall is a good time to plant them. Always buy top-grade bulbs from Holland that are at least a healthy one and a half inches in size. My personal preference among all the varieties of tulips is the Darwin hybrid.

While I am on the subject, you can prolong the bloom of your flowers in the fall by hosing off the frost with water in the early morning.

Cover your roses, of course, but not too soon. Let them harden as long as possible. The new styrofoam cones are wonderful, although putting them on too soon produces mildew, due to dampness and shade, and a continuation of plant growth, which is generated by the higher temperature of the enclosure. I always wait to cover roses until there is absolutely no chance of warm temperatures recurring.

If your tulips are up from last fall, let their leaves wither and brown away. Don't cut them off, or you will deprive the bulbs of nutrition for next year. Just plant summer flowers among the dormant tulips. The tulip draws its food from its leaves and stores it in the bulb for next spring's growth.

# Trees and Shrubs

ACCORDING TO the National Tree Conference, trees perfect in every respect are valued at about $7 per square inch of trunk in cross section. To get the value of a tree, square the radius, multiply by 3.1416, and then multiply the result by $7. Thus a tree of 20-inch diameter would be valued at $2,199. In business, if something this expensive were in need of repair, it would get immediate attention. Why not your beautiful trees?

## General Care of Trees

In the early spring, check the trees carefully for dead limbs. Look, too, for cracks at the crotches. If these aren't too high or too large, you or your gardener can prune and paint and possibly guy the branches. Don't take chances and break your neck if the job is too risky and hard; call a qualified company to do the work. Its tree climbers are insured and paid to take risks. You might also have the tree-service people fertilize your giants by root feeding, especially if the trees are surrounded by cement walks, driveways, or terraces. Believe me, it's worth it. The tree-service companies can be found in the yellow pages of the telephone book, or your neighbor or a friend might know of one that's reliable. Always get two or three estimates unless you can call a park superintendent, city forester, or golf-course superintendent who will recommend a company. Never, definitely never, hire the "expert" who knocks on your door or telephones you.

Keep this in mind about other yard and lawn services, too. The exception is when your city or villages informs you that Dutch elm disease has been discovered in one of your elms. Then the tree has to be taken down either by town employees at a reasonable cost to you or by a company they recommended.

When the tree men come, ask them to show you how to fertilize your smaller trees, and what to use. Usually the needs of trees with diameters of three or four inches can be satisfied with a one-pound coffee can full of 10-10-10, 10-6-4, or a similar fertilizer, distributed evenly in holes punched every two feet around the circle where leaves from the outside branches fall. Make the holes a foot deep and one to two inches in diameter with a rod or crowbar. Never fertilize next to the trunk.

When a tree has been transplanted there will be very little top growth during its first year because the major adjustment is in the root zone. The shock of transplanting is great, and the tree must adapt itself to the new soil, a different position in the sunlight, and its new environment, even though this may be just a matter of a mile or so from its place of origin. New roots must grow to replace those cut off in the balling process. Since trees feed through their roots, it would be useless to feed the tree heavily during this time. It's like putting salt on a wound. We must first give the tree a chance to heal and grow new feeder roots so it can utilize amounts of fertilizer. I'll compare this to a golf enthusiast coming out of a hospital after major surgery or a heart attack. Can he go out and shoot the same game that he did before he went into the hospital? Of course not. It takes a long time for him to come back to normal, and the same applies to a transplanted tree.

If you own even a single American elm, have the tree-service people spray it—before your neighbor spring-cleans her windows and before too many birds return. Late fall to April is best.

## Care of Elm Trees

In 1929, an ordinary freighter from Holland docked in New York with a full load of elm logs. In this load of still-green wood, unknown to anyone, was a destructive fungus that causes the devastating Dutch elm disease. The disease is transmitted by the European bark beetle, brownish-black and about one-eighth inch long. This onetime visitor now resides throughout the United States and eastern Canada, breeding under the bark of dead elms. After the young beetles fly off to feed on healthy elm trees, minute spores from the fungus in the dead tree, carried on their bodies, rub off and enter borings or wounds in the healthy bark, where the spores develop into the fungus that does the actual killing of the tree. The fungus enters the sapwood and clogs the vascular system of the elm; the tree dies; beetles breed; and spores get carried away to another elm. Symptoms of a diseased elm are wilting and, as in the fall, a prominent show of yellow leaves, usually on the top of the tree (called flagging), which progresses downward. Most elms die the same season they are attacked, sometimes in a few weeks. The beetles like to feed on the new terminal growth of the twig crotches. If you have American elms and have the slightest doubt about their health, ask the opinion of a tree expert or the public works department of your town. Better yet, cut off six inches of a branch of half-inch diameter that has just wilted, wrap it in wax paper or aluminum foil, and send it to the recommended agency. After the specimen is cultured you will be informed of the health of your elms. Be sure the branch is not completely dead; if it is, the fungus is inactive and impossible to culture.

Keeping your elms healthy requires sanitation and spraying for an extended time. Clean them by pruning dead and unnecessary branches. Also, immediately cut down and burn all infected trees. Spray your trees in the dormant period between late fall and early spring before the birds return. This has to be done by properly equipped tree experts; they use a spray that generally contains DDT. Interestingly, in northern and western Europe, Dutch elm disease is now only a minor nuisance, mainly because of sanitation practices.

In my many years of watching the Dutch elm disease slowly eliminate the American elm, I have observed that the lone elm, in comparative isolation, so to speak, and the elms with lots of space between them are much less likely to be hit by the disease than those in crowded tree ghettos. Therefore, it may become necessary to eliminate many elms in these overpopulated areas in order to save a few for posterity. Meanwhile, the federal government is currently spending a niggardly quarter of a million dollars in research every year.

Many alleged cures have been prescribed (some, such as aspirin, iodine, vinegar, and crankcase oil, were ridiculous). More "cures" pop up every year. But so far there is no cure, only control—by sanitation and dormant spraying.

It is sad to note that when the scourge of the elms first started in the 1930's in our biggest city, it was quickly controlled by sanitation. Then, for some reason, this practice ceased, and now the disease is a national calamity.

As usual, public apathy and political confusion, plus the tremendous dispersion of the disease, have affected attempts at any control program. There seems to be no cure for either this "disease" or the elm disease. It is the great American tragedy of present times, the slow disappearance of another species, the American elm—a noble tree, whose symmetrical beauty resembles the graceful shape of a wineglass—a tree that dignifies any home with its majestic bearing and grandeur, and any street with its dense shade and beauty. This is a tree that must be saved or we shall lose a part of our heritage, for trees such as these are not luxury, but a necessity.

## Planting Trees and Shrubs

October is the time to plant trees, when plants are entering their period of dormancy. Take the whole family along to the nursery. You'll have fun and, most important of all, you'll be able to select the specimens personally. Years later when the trees are tall and shading you from the hot sun, your youngsters will get a kick out of remembering that once they could almost lift the tree with one hand. Incidentally, a tree planted in your yard is a contribution not only to your home and family, but to the entire community as well.

Landscaping always should be simple and uncluttered. One well-placed excellent tree will have more impact, especially when mature, than many haphazardly planted shrubs. A small yard with an enormous variety of shrubs looks like a retail nursery.

Plan your landscaping to include the perspective of the house along with the natural features of the yard. They belong together and your plan should make them harmonious. Sometimes, though, you will have to compromise a personal preference in individual plants to achieve the overall theme. Some things you may want out of sight. If so, use trees or shrubbery to conceal telephone boxes, rain spouts, garbage cans, garden and tool sheds, and anything else you want to hide, like a compost pile.

Nursery stock is grown in fertile soil, and in well-spaced rows to receive maximum sunlight. The trees are properly fertilized and shaped from the beginning so they will have sturdy trunks and tops rather than skinny heights. Whenever necessary they are sprayed, and they are transplanted many times to develop a compact fibrous root system.

If you buy trees or shrubs from a distant area (often at cheaper prices), you are asking for trouble because you don't know their origin, hardiness, or the food deficiencies of their soils; nor will they be acclimated to your local conditions. You will be much better off to select a reliable nearby nursery and stick with it.

Beware of extraordinary claims and "new discoveries" and bargains—you never get something for nothing. But if you do take a flier, remember there can be a big difference between what you see in a direct-mail brochure and what you get. The picture shown is usually of a full-grown tree; what you get sometimes is a starting plant only a few inches high.

While planning your landscaping, ask yourself (or someone else) how much maintenance is required. Then make your selections.

Avoid trees whose limbs break easily or have unattractive litter, such as messy fruits, nuts, and seed pods. If you are building a swimming pool, locate the deciduous trees at a distance so leaves are not constantly falling or blowing into the water.

The wrapping of trees has a purpose. Transplanted trees will usually face in a different direction than they did in the nursery.

The shady side may now be the sunny side, and the tree can get sun scald. The wrapping also keeps the trunk warm in the fall, when the sap flows on the sunny side. If there is a quick freeze, the sap freezes, and the bark breaks and splits the cambium layer. So wrap your new trees.

During any large-scale building operation in the yard, all trees should be protected with boards to prevent damage to the trunks by machines. The contractor should look after this, although you may need to insist. Tag each tree with its common and Latin name and then record it and its age in your gardening book; if you ever sell your home, the new owner will appreciate these identifications. Read up on the trees you already have and the ones you personally select. You'll be an authority. And when your neighbor asks what you're planting, you can state authoritatively and proudly, "An *Acer rubrum*" (or whatever it is).

Late summer and early fall are the best times to pick out fruit and berry trees for spring planting. Fruit trees are generally the exception to the fall-planting rule. They alone, of all trees, should be planted in early spring. Late in September they are full and ripe, and by going out to the nursery you can see how the fruit looks, what type you want for your home, and which variety does best in your vicinity. Just think of the harvest you'll have at your door in a few years. You can encourage your wife with a new hobby, too: the berries made into your own brand-name jellies and preserves. And she, in this pleasant give and take, might suggest a hobby for you: homemade wines and liqueurs.

During the Depression and Prohibition nearly everyone made his own booze. My father, who considered himself quite a connoisseur of homemade wines, made a batch from chokecherries. For some reason it went bad and my parents threw it in the pig trough. Well, the chickens got to it and the results were hilarious. Did you ever see a rooster fight on a farm? It's a funny sight. But in this case it wasn't rooster against rooster. The hens attacked! The poor roosters, not knowing what madness had come over the hens, and being a little tipsy themselves, ran helter-skelter through the farmyard trying to escape the drunks. You know, the eggs a few weeks later tasted funny—a little like port.

So far we've talked mostly about the homeowner doing his own landscaping. There is another way: hiring a reputable landscape contractor who also has a design service. But if you can afford the prices, the ideal would be to have a professional landscape architect do the job. Look at it this way: do you ask a carpenter to build your home? Of course not. You start with a set of architect's plans. Do the same with the rest of your property. Ask for bids, too. There could be a broad price range for landscaping, but a rule-of-thumb figure is 10 percent of the cost of house and property. You don't have quite that much in the checking account this month? Well, here is something people don't realize. Landscaping can be financed by an F.H.A. home-improvement loan. In this day of easy credit, I can think of no finer way for the homeowner to get himself in the hole than with a properly landscaped home. And there's another consideration: as your home depreciates with age, your plants appreciate in value.

## Poisonous Plants

During summer many of us like to make a trek to the woods. Walking is a lost art, and more of it should be done. However, when walking in the woods or looking for a lost golf ball in the rough, beware of poison ivy. It is the most irritating of all itches, and the most unnecessary of all skin afflictions. Although there are other plants that cause contact dermatitis, poison ivy and poison oak are the worst. Both produce irritation. Dr. Albert Slepyan, noted dermatologist and professor of dermatology at the University of Illinois, has some advice: "Poison ivy is a mockingbird plant whose leaves sometimes resembles those of the white oak, the basswood, or the sassafras. The plant has a great ability to vary the shape and form of its leaflets. However, it always has three leaves growing together; let them be." Amen. Avoid them also when they're being burned.

A few plants and parts of plants not usually thought of as poisonous are the castor bean, foxglove, oak acorns, lily of the valley, the red berries of the female yew, and horse chestnuts. There's also deadly nightshade. All these and many others can cause severe sickness and possibly death if chewed and swallowed. Beware of them in the woods, and make sure they don't grow in your garden, especially if you have young children. Tell your children not to pick berries and warn them never, never to eat them.

At my first golf course I grew the magnificent, fast-growing castor bean, much to the pleasure of the members. It was the center and showpiece of a beautiful round flower garden between the first and tenth tees for many years, until I found out its seeds contained a powerful poison.

# The Future: Some Predictions

THE LAST of our chores is done and the time has come to relax. Let's open a bottle of imported beer (you deserve it) and contemplate the future.

What will the future be like for the homeowner? Let's pick 1984. Unlike George Orwell's *1984,* our year will be a utopia for the homeowner. Here are my predictions.

All home lawns will be automatically irrigated through nonmetallic pipe. There will be herbicides that control *all* the weeds. They will be absolutely safe to use and easy to apply, and only one application will be necessary. This will not be the case with insects because, as one insect is controlled, another one, a minor pest before, will take over.

Insects will be more and more a problem as mutated species develop resistance to controls and as now unfamiliar insects come from far-distant geographical areas.

Fewer numbers of fungi will attack our grass, not so much because of new wonder fungicides to control turf diseases as because of better and stronger strains of grass. A great need exists in the transition areas (see page 14) for a grass that will do well through the entire growing season. Ben Warren, a turf grower, makes this prophecy:

> The next five to ten years should see several bluegrass selections that rival and probably displace Merion as the outstanding bluegrass in its area of adoption. There should be strains available for such specific uses as short mowing, shady locations, and heavy traffic, plus strains for definite geographical locations.

One fertilizer of the future will be placed not on top of the grass, but under it. Although it will be incorporated into the soil when the seedbed is prepared, as is done now, this slow-releasing fertilizer will last for *several years* before having to be replenished on top of the grass. With this discovery, most of the trouble and expense to the greenhorn homeowner during the first few years of his new lawn will be gone.

What about mowing? Well, my crystal ball predicts good news for the homeowner. An excellent growth retardant will be marketed by 1984, and the homeowner won't have to mow as often as he does now. Strains of dwarf grass will also be discovered.

As for the mowers of tomorrow, two wiser and more experienced gentlemen than I have answers. First, C. A. Liversey, an executive of a firm making home lawn machinery, states, "Engines for mowers are being improved and more power is now packaged in a smaller, lighter unit. Electricity is gaining in popularity as a power source for homeowners. If in the future more efficient batteries for the storage of electrical power are developed, these could become a principal power source because of their convenience and lack of mechanical maintenance."

My good friend Dr. Jim Watson, an agronomist from Minneapolis, says:

> Equipment for grooming and maintaining the home lawn of the future will be more versatile and will . . . develop in accordance with total lawn care requirements. Hence, one unit will perform a number of functions, and equally important, the job will be accomplished in substantially less time.
>
> Further away, yet within range of today's technology, it seems likely that the homeowner will be able to devote as much, or

as little, time to the operation of future lawn care equipment as he may choose. Lawn care will have eliminated the drudgery and tedium sometimes associated with today's maintenance practices.

What about the weather? The *Farmer's Almanac* will be just as popular and just as correct as it's always been. However, forecasts derived from satellite information will be more accurate. Rainmaking techniques will be more advanced, and the time will come when it will be possible to make rain on areas that are very dry or drought-stricken. But rainmaking will be tightly controlled and will be resorted to only in emergencies. After all, moisture made to fall in one area must be stolen from another. Moreover, Mrs. Levy and Mrs. Jones might sue if unexpected man-made rainwater was added to the drinks being served at their lawn party.

I predict that special refrigeration techniques will be able to keep landscape stock fresh and dormant for long periods. This will enable the landscape contractor to deliver nursery stock by refrigerated vans, with no danger that it might succumb to the heat between the time it's dug out of the ground and the time it's planted. A way already has been discovered to cool sod by a vacuum process, reducing its temperature so low that the sod is delivered to the homeowner fresh and green on the hottest day.

We are all concerned about the threat of air pollution to human health, but not everyone is aware that air pollution is just as harmful to grass and trees as it is to us. It's my belief that the problem will be solved only when the government regulates construction of power plants, factories, and industries, specifying certain distances between them and limiting the size and number in any given locality. However, the solution hangs on the use of "clean" atomic power for our homes, cars, and factories, thus eliminating all contaminants. Greater attention to environmental matters will benefit both the grass and the man behind the mower.

I also see an end to the solid asphalt ghettos and a return of nature to the cities. Plans for the renewal of our cities will include, along with man's architectural achievements, the splendor of grass and trees and flowers. There will even come a time when developers and wise city fathers, touched by love of the outdoors (or by plain old common sense), will include not only places for schools, churches, and shopping centers in their housing developments, but also a little bit of forest or woodland for each community. I hope, too, that in the ugly process of destruction for progress they will set aside a portion of wilderness where birds can sing, animals can hide, and wild flowers can grow; that a little bit of countryside will be left untouched where little boys can once more run and play and dream, where there will be room to build huts, make slingshots, and whittle Indian whistles. I wish for this with all my heart.

# Index

# Index

## About the Author

PAUL N. VOYKIN was born in 1931 in Saskatoon, Saskatchewan, and spent his childhood in the family homestead at Red Pheasant and the nearby prairie communities of Langham and Blaine Lake. His professional career began with W. "Pops" Brinkworth at the golf course in Jasper National Park and continued at Lethbridge, Alberta, and Olympia Fields, a southern suburb of Chicago. In 1961 he became superintendent at Briarwood Country Club and in 1963, his "proudest moment," a U.S. citizen. He is a hockey fan, plays an 11-handicap game of golf, and has one unusual handicap, an allergy to soil molds, which includes several species of grass. Mr. Voykin is vice-president of the Midwest Golf Course Superintendents Association and has given talks on turf, flowers, and golf course administration in San Diego and at Purdue University and various turf clinics. He is married and the father of four daughters and a son.

PRINTED IN U.S.A.